PETROL, BAIT, AMMO & ICE

PETROL, BAIT, AMMO' & ICE

• • • • • • • • • • • • • • • • • • • •

H.G. NELSON

with a foreword by *ROY SLAVEN*
illustrated by *REG MOMBASSA*

MACMILLAN
Pan Macmillan Australia

First published 1996 in Pan by Pan Macmillan Australia Pty Limited
St Martins Tower, 31 Market Street, Sydney

Reprinted 1996 (twice)

National Library of Australia
cataloguing-in-publication data:
Nelson, H.G.
Petrol, bait, ammo & ice.
ISBN 0 330 35790 5.
1. Sports - Humour. 2. Sports - Anecdotes. I. Title.
796.0207

Printed in Australia by Australian Print Group

Francis Bacon at Port Hedland.

Foreword

● ● ● ● ● ● ● ● ● ● ● ● ●

I was browsing through my splendid volume of the collected works of Gerard Manley Hopkins just the other day, reacquainting myself with 'The Windhover'—*I caught this morning morning's minion*, etc—and couldn't help be reminded that the master poet wished that at all times his work be read aloud. *Take breath and read me with the ears* was the instruction and so it was while I was in the backyard bellowing one of the 'terrible' sonnets that it occurred to me that the same rule could well apply to the master works of H.G. Nelson which appear in this volume. To read H.G. is to be propelled through both the Australian landscape and, just as importantly, the Australian timescape. As for landscape, **I don't think any Australian writer can transport a reader so effortlessly from the inside of an EH Holden Special with the windows down on a hot summer's day on the open road between Quorn and Hawker with the radio picking up the call of the sixth dog race at Gawler while the Golden Guide turns its upturned edges brown on the dashboard, to the lonely silence of the MCG on a mid-winter's Saturday afternoon an hour after the final hooter has rung down on a Carlton victory over Collingwood where the silence is only occasionally broken by the rustle of a program using the power of draught to force its way through an advertising hoarding.** H.G. takes us over and through Australia.

As for the timescape, H.G.'s language travels backwards and forwards simultaneously. To read him aloud is to force the tongue and glottis and back palate to visit the mouths of those whose task it is to convert visual imagery into abstract symbols at speed. And so the

● ● ● ●

mouths of Des Hoysted, Ken Callander, Ken Howard, Frank Hyde and Alan McGilvray and others can be visited, but with a richness of irony none of them could ever attain. And so within this timescape H.G. can use the language sensibilities of the disappointed punter of the late 1940s to describe the impact of the Internet upon the Australian recording industry; can take the language of the track and apply it to Brett Whiteley's struggle to shock in the manner of Francis Bacon; can show us how Ray 'Rabbits' Warren would tackle the thorny issue of gene shears and its relationship to the elimination of left-handedness in world professional tennis; and can show us Ray Connolly introducing Aung San Suu Kyi to Boutros Boutros-Ghali after the Sumayet Payakarun–Lester Ellis bout, 'Baby' John Burgess visiting the Tate Gallery, 'King' Wally Lewis getting 'Dishead' Dowling's thoughts on the balance of payments crisis, and Bert Newton's and 'Weary' Dunlop's collected impressions on the Second Law of Thermodynamics and the Arrow of Time. H.G.'s style is, therefore, a linguistic collage requiring an ear for detail both unusual and unique.

But it's H.G.'s passionate obsession with detail that provides the rich spice to the flavour. Why is it that sport is so often let down by its rules? Why are there so many grey areas in sports administration? Why can't the blight that is LBW be cleaned up? When is an AFL player caught with the ball? What is the rugby league scrum all about? Why is it still there? Why aren't rugby league footballers forced to smoke on the paddock and therefore endorse the sponsor's product? Why is Bobby Simpson still there? If you had a multimillion dollar enterprise, would you let Arko be at the helm? What is the relationship between Kerry Packer and rugby league? Is it healthy? Why should Fitzroy merge when tens of thousands of supporters wish otherwise? Why should so much paper space and air time be given to Fuzzy Zoeler, Peter Senior, Laughing Lee, Ben Crenshaw and Arnie's Army? What does the Great White Shark tell us about Australia? What is wrong with our New Pat? Where is the language school that trained Simon Crean and Martin Ferguson? Should Australia have a space industry? What is the difference between the Australian Labor Party and the Liberal Party? What is it that attracts the eye to Bouveng, Skarden and Vowles? What do Dean Brown and Denver Beanland have in common? Who is winning the war between Holden and Ford? These are just some of the issues that H.G. covers in this collection.

But to read H.G. reveals a working knowledge of the driving forces within the Australian community. Most will look at an attractive Tom Ramsey article and take it at face value. H.G. is one of the very few who can see the other darker rhythms at work, guiding the brain that guides the hand that ends up a piece on the newspaper page with Tom's byline attached. So, too, with Steve Crawley and Ray Chesterton and Phil Tresidder and all the others whose job it is to further the dubious relationship between sport and money.

On a final note, I have much to thank for bumping into H.G. all those years ago. Having spent thousands of hours with him on air I can honestly say that the freshness and brilliance that are his style have not dimmed with time. If anything, the contrary is true. As sport and its attendant world become more and more muddled and sullied in proportion to their distance from their amateur beginnings, so the need for the genius of H.G. Nelson increases. When we met he forced me to run faster and in directions I would never have thought possible, and there was a time when foolishly I thought I may have been able to catch up to him.

**NOT SO. There is only one H.G. Nelson and I was lucky enough to find him, and luckier still that he chose me to work with. So take a deep breath and read him with your ears.
ROY SLAVEN**

Preface

● ● ● ● ● ● ● ● ● ● ●

I'm on record as saying I don't read anything unless I have written it myself, but I've gone out of my way to make an exception with PETROL, BAIT, AMMO & ICE.

Look, I'd be lying if I said I have read it all. *I haven't*. But I've gathered from listening to work-mates in the fashion caper and people talking at traffic lights in the backseats of expensive European cars that this book grips you. It gives you support where you need it and comes at you like a size ten Versace frock. All this without a hint of the unsightly wedgie. And that's a big rap.

People around the world have been drawn to PETROL, BAIT, AMMO & ICE whenever it has spilled out of my handbag on a continental dance floor under the mirror ball when romance was the only topic on the agenda. Total strangers have given it a good hard geek and like what they've seen. **It's drawn a lot more comment, for instance, than my spare pair of Bendon smalls or my date book (which is a *very* lively read).**

Underwear lovers, I love to get up late and have a big break-fast of a low cal cream-cheese-and-chives bagel and a half a cup of black coffee. To top off a huge feast like this I have to lie back on the ottoman, relax, have a fiddle and give H.G.'s handi-work a red-hot shufti. I suggest you do the same.

ELLE MACPHERSON
(cafe proprietor and writer)

THIS BOOK HAS BEEN THROUGH A LONG BAKE IN THE OVEN
before being turned out on the cooling tray for you to savour its
aroma. As well as those listed in the introduction, I want to thank
SANDRA HORTH from the design shed at Pan Macmillan for an extra
heave in getting this sponge cake out of the oven and into the current
form. Sandra has done a match-winning job in creating a way for my
prose to be decorated by Reg's best on-ground illustrations. Sandra saw
the job of designing PETROL, BAIT, AMMO & ICE as both a sporting
challenge and summertime fun. With this improbable but wonderful
double she has made the sum of these parts into a much greater whole.

There would be no book without the typists, who must hate clowns
like me who swan in with a lot of poorly presented material. Double
thanks to JULIE NEKICH and JODIE O'SHEA for their patience and
typing skills which have made sense of my manuscript and my desire to
overwrite in spidery long hand with failing biros on anything that looks
halfway finished.

A number of these sprays surfaced for air for the first time in print.
I am indebted to the following magazines and newspapers who gave me a
chance to write for them and in doing so helped keep the economic wolf
howling on a leash and away from savaging the flyscreen at the back
door. In particular, I want to thank the Sydney Morning Herald, the Good
Weekend, the Sunday Age, the ABC Cricket Season 1995/6 (published by
Gore & Osment Publications Pty Ltd), the Telegraph Mirror (née the Daily
Telegraph), Modern Motor (RIP), Plenty (RIP), Inside Sport, Penthouse,
the Broncos Magazine, the Bulletin, and Qantas Inflight Magazine, who
all rang and asked for a few words and hopefully got more than they
bargained for. Plus thanks to the following organisations who took it
from me in the flesh: East Sydney Tech, the Adelaide Fringe Festival, the
Adelaide Festival, the Comedy Unit at the ABC (Debates), 100% Mambo,
the Open Family and the Screen Producers Association of Australia.

Thanks to these former employers for allowing me to collect all
these diverse performances and bang them between the covers. Without
your help there would be bugger-all to look back on.

And finally, as I keep my fingers crossed in the hope that I haven't
left anybody off the list (if I have, I'm obviously thinking of you a lot),
I would like to acknowledge the tremendous contribution to my whole
working experience over the last ten years from JOHN DOYLE. John,
without knowing just how, has helped immensely, both directly and
indirectly, in the creation of PETROL, BAIT, AMMO & ICE.

Acknowledgements

Introduction

My very good friends, it has been ten years since Roy and I pulled on the shorts and pushed off down at the very deep end of the pool and began making those tricky hard yards, going the grope, applying the squirrel, laying on a bit of nut, bagging the hard ones on the turn and shouting above the horrible din that passed in those days for informed sports commentary in this nation.

When you have had an extremely successful career spanning the decades since the war in meat, meat products, meat marketing, home-slaughtering, rural banking and the hair care sciences, all produced under the banner of the Slaven Nelson Group of Companies, it is hard to strike out in a totally new direction and snare from the tee that elusive smidgen of success.

Roy and I took an enormous risk going into the fickle and fraught world of the media and, in particular, sports commentating. We were driven to do it by a lot of old clowns pogged down on radio and television who were screaming sport at us like hapless water buffaloes stuck in the mud waiting for the safari to arrive with the elephant gun to put them out of their misery. Hopefully we pulled up in the ute within shooting distance just in time.

You could put it down to mid-life crisis. You could claim it was sheer stupidity. But **in the final analysis ten years ago there was an opening in the world of sport bellowing out to be filled in and we were on hand at the top of the trench with the shovels**. That crack in the sports landscape was just wide enough to let Roy and me wriggle through.

When we began circulating at speed, scraping the door handles off with a boot full of dodgy dynamite, operating at a full fifteen decibels above the rest of the pack, going in hard on pillows and booting show ponies up the date, we thought we might last two months before the referees at the ABC blew the very loud whistle and ordered us off for an early shower.

That those with their hands on the ABC levers put the whistle away for so long has amazed me and is surely, my very good friends, a savage indictment on broadcasting standards in this nation as we head towards the turn of the century.

Now that ten years have elapsed it's time to pause at the top of the straight, look back and reflect on this long, twisty, mud-filled, pot-holed, Russ Hinze-designed road that has been *This Sporting Life* on Triple J and now flowers as *Club Buggery* on ABC TV. Over the past decade Roy Slaven and I have been asked to talk at pie nights, coaching clinics, national press clubs, lingerie fund-raising parades, weddings, christenings, auctions for old sporting identities' testimonials, fête openings, prize nights, club best-and-fairest do's. We have been asked to say a few ill-chosen words before hurling the bottle at the boat and seeing the new tub on the slide, as well as preparing and presenting our regular weekly media commitments. It's from the rubbish that has been discarded along this long roadside that *PETROL, BAIT, AMMO & ICE* has been recycled.

This collection neatly puts the last few years on this side of the flooded creek and clears the way forward for the seed to be stuck into the dirt on the other. Seed that will hopefully bloom into a second decade. You, the reader, travel over a Bailey bridge with one section laid out by Roy, the other by yours truly.

Preparing this collection has brought back many, many marvellous memories of magnificent grand final wins, of great Lithgow Cups, of impossible-to-forget State of Origin clashes, of great horses like Rooting King, of spine-tingling one day cricket finals, of playing away at the All England, of players like Stomper Stains and so on, but more importantly it has focused the mind on a tremendous number of low moments in human dignity and outright farce created by players, officials, administrators, TV presenters, radio commentators and reporters. This has been the fuel of our work. All Roy and I did was provide the match.

The dud lingers a lot longer than the things that went right. The stench of rotten fruit is a lot more pungent than the ripe peach. The smell of decay is a lot more memorable in the retelling.

And so to our craft.

There is bugger-all to it. We kept it simple, very bloody simple. Longwinded, sure—this is an essential ingredient. When you have had a red-hot go at any issue, back up and stab it some more. In ten years on the spike of commentating Roy and I have never actually drilled any issue completely to death to our total satisfaction. The problems presented by the Great White Shark, Greg Norman, and Aussie Joe Bugner have demanded our best pace attack, but there is so much more of the story yet to tell. There was always another squeeze of the lemon, even when we leave the scene. Some might not think so, but you're only limited by your imagination.

Another stick of gelignite in our boot is we make the serious trivial and the trivial serious. The more serious the issue, the more it can be trivialised. And the same is true in the opposite direction. Other handy hints: go everywhere but stay at home as often as you can. On air, know everyone intimately but try like hell in real life to meet no-one unless you are absolutely sure you can keep bagging them after you've gripped their hand and had a fiddle. With these simple guidelines you should be able to unravel the rest of the act yourself and still amaze friends with your party turns.

And so to teary time as I let the lower lip droop and splash the boots with tears of joy mixed in equal part with tears of sadness at the passing of time, the passing of players and the passing of great moments.

This project has been pulled together through several sets of very safe hands. At the top of the dig, I would be an idiot to myself if I didn't thank 'the Inflatable Pig on a Bendy Stick Network', Triple J. **A long time ago the ABC's 'Yoof Network' gave a couple of suckers with a very slim idea an enormous break and allowed them to call the 1986 Rugby League Grand Final. At the death the Eels snuck away from the Dogs 4–2**. Ray Warren finished his last call for Channel 10 that day with the immortal words, 'And so it's farewell from Pricey, the Cro and the Rabbit.' See what I mean about the dud lingering longer than the swift?

Then, in an even greater miracle, our very dear friends in Triple J management left us alone to get on with it every Saturday afternoon. Largely, I suspect, because they didn't have a clue about what we were up to and more importantly had no idea how to whip it into shape before plucking up the courage to show us the door.

This effort was even more impressive given that at the time they didn't appear to give an overripe, fruit fly-blown, split paw-paw on the drop from the vine about sport or any physical activity apart from an excitable late night rhumba.

Throughout our whole time at the Inflatable Pig, Mark Kennedy has been our long suffering producer who deployed his marvellous talents under the nom de radio Might Mike Shy. Blowing his cover in this cruel and totally callous manner does give me a chance to acknowledge his wonderful ability at capturing in sound our garbled instructions. His outstanding efforts have provided a fantastic aural backdrop for a long run of hastily cobbled-together bits of script and rubbish we dared to call a radio program. His work has contributed a powerful third prong and just as the Beatles had George Martin, *This Sporting Life* has been lucky enough to have Mark Kennedy.

In the last three years ABC TV has found space in their schedules for us to wriggle about lewdy-style on the box, firstly on a Monday night with a punk current affairs show called *This Sporting Life*. Then in 1995, after a couple of proving flights to the lower altitudes, they allowed us to light a wick under the candle and blast off with a full

Friday night interstellar catastrophe called *Club Buggery*.

Roy and I are indebted to the Comedy Unit under the baton of Michael Shrimpton and producers Ted Robinson and Mark Fitzgerald for giving the panel the time to make the tricky transition from the crystal set on the mantle piece to the crystal bucket aglow in the corner of your games room. I thank them for taking a chance on a couple of lads who liked to burble on in a big way and for giving them a go at making pictures.

The team at Pan Macmillan is the next cab off the rank and I need to thank DEBORAH CALLAGHAN for getting me involved with Pan by suggesting I launch Tom Carroll's book, *The Wave Within*.

Once on board the Pan bus I have to thank AMANDA HEMMINGS for making wonderful sense from a cardboard box full of rubbish, and NIKKI CHRISTER for guiding this effort past the most obvious rocks, reefs and fins circling in the water up ahead even though the motor was dead and the oars were back in the clubhouse.

REG MOMBASSA very kindly opened the bottom drawer in the artistic tallboy out back in the shed. He said, 'Go for your life, sport,' and then let me rummage around for days in the black and whites. Reg can rustle up an artistic idea full of grunt, poke and merit that smacks you between the eyes like a blow from a carefully aimed ice-cold dead mullet.

It's in the quiet moments when Reg gets a chance to relax away from the open cut of commercialism and has a go at something more traditional you realise that not only can he pull a pencil across a blank sheet of paper but he can stack on the Taubmans better than most.

And finally and by no means last picked there is RAMPAGING ROY SLAVEN. It is well documented that Roy picked me up when I was down and out on the blub, finding me derelict on a mid-winter's Thursday night behind the grandstand at the Dapto dog track. This was the second best thing that has happened to me. Roy saw something in that bundle of mess that I refused to see in myself. A glimmer of hope maybe. A bloke just having a run of outs. An idiot who had gone for one too many Burtons. Who knows? He didn't stop for a minute. It's true

xvi

that at the time I didn't like being kicked up the date in public. I didn't like being told to stare into the very large mirror he was carrying and have a good hard look at myself. But that is exactly what I did. Roy turned me around. He got me over my addiction to hair care remedies and pointed me forward once again. I can never thank him enough.

When, just after the war, we began making the hard yards together in the hair care caper with those ideas about meat that butchers still only dream about, it was a downhill run. I have been lucky enough to have Roy up the business end of the tandem bike ever since. **He doesn't realise that I have my feet up at the back on the handlebars as he does the hard work making light of those country kilometres. He never screams as we make those tough climbs, 'Put in, H.G.' I'm up the back on the bludge taking in the sights, writing to loved ones, chatting with kiddies and working on my Spring Carnival doubles selections while he actually 'promotes' the machine.**

Over the past ten years I can say with absolute authority that I have only touched pedals when passing a political dignitary, a member of the media or one of the wallet-openers at the ABC. Roy, I couldn't have done it without you at the front handlebars, pal. Thanks heaps.

But in the end none of it would have been possible without you, fun-loving Australians who were prepared to listen to a couple of old boof-heads talking about things they knew very little about and then were prepared to wriggle around under the doona to indicate that you were alive when the ratings experts pulled up in the panel van out front. Thanks very much for waving the underpants in approval at the appropriate moments when they were looking in your direction. Thanks for turning us on whenever we have dared to get on the bleat.

Now off you shoot and have a dip at PETROL, BAIT, AMMO & ICE.

● ● ● ● ● ● ● ● ● ● ● ● ● ● H.G. NELSON ● ● ●

ON THE GRUNT:

Winning At Wimbledon

There is no finer sound in all of sport than to arrive at the gates of Wimbledon just after the off and hear the silence of the drama unfolding on the centre court punctuated by a lot of loud grunts and growls. The sound of teeth taming the ball.

1990 will be remembered forever as the year the grunt returned. Sure, a lot of people think a good grunt is unseemly and it somehow lowers the tone of the caper. What a lot of soggy old rope.

AUSTRALIA HAS TURNED OUT GREAT PLAYERS AND GREAT GRUNTERS, SUCH AS EDO, NEWK, J.A., DENTY, HOADIE, MISTER MUSCLES, THE ROCKHAMPTON ROCKET, WOODIE, FIREY and RUFFO, to name just a handful off the top of the head. But is the grunt game as good today as it was yesterday? Frankly, today's growlers are amateurs and wouldn't be allowed out to play if they met any of the big names of yesteryear. Kenny Rosewall could terrify once he got the throat lubricated with a couple of sips of tea, while Newk reduced many an opponent to a heap of jelly when he drew back the lips and gave a low 'grrrrrr' as soon as the umpy said, 'Play ball.'

And who is to say that the current poor standing of Australians in the world rankings is due solely to the fact that we as a nation have forgotten how to lay on a bit of a growl?

The serve and volley caper, for mine, has always been a brawl with two greats slugging it out toe to toe, head to head, *mano y mano*, armed with nothing but a racquet, a couple of balls, their bare teeth and the sound of their own voice. Wimbledon itself has always been a fortnight of fight on grass instead of on canvas. Sure, it has had a veneer of civilisation, an illusion of decorum created by the strawberries and clotted cream on offer in the hospitality tent and by the string net draped at the midway point of the court instead of round the edge as in the boxing and wrestling caper. But that veneer, which has always been paper-thin, was punctured this year by a few growlers and grunters who have

I WAS A MESS OF SHEEP'S BRAINS DONE UP IN A WHITE SAUCE WHEN THE NEWS HIT ME, LIKE A KNEE TO THE CRUETS, THAT THE GRUNT HAD RETURNED TO WOMEN'S TENNIS AT WIMBLEDON. I LOVE TO SEE THIS NEW BREED WITH A BIG SERVE, BIG VOLLEY AND BIG GRUNT OUT ON CENTRE COURT HOWLING THEIR WAY TO THE BIG TIN PLATE ON OFFER ● ● ● ● ● ● ● ● ●

brought a bit of the traditional softening-up back to the Centre Court.

For years I have been pleading with the All England brains trust to do away with the net and just let them at it like animals, growling and grunting until one got the upper hand and the ref said enough.

AND WHO IS TO SAY WE WOULDN'T SEE BETTER TENNIS?

1

LICKING HONEY OFF A RUSTY NAIL: 1995, Rugby League's Best Year Yet . . . .

● ● ● ● ● IT WAS SO EASY DURING 1995,
rugby league's year of living dopily, to just bag. The
house of cards that was the code came crashing
down as a very big and a very tangy Cheese
carrying a bag full of cash shouted across the
pay TV and free-to-air channels,
'Hey, blokes, want a fat slice of the gorgonzola?'

SATAN'S PROD – the quest begins

Welcome to this magnificent occasion, the unofficial Grand Final Breakfast for 1995, where we as a nation begin to go delirious with enjoyment in celebration of the Festival of the Boot Part One, namely the Rugby League Grand Final and the ongoing Search for Satan's Prod Buried at the Crossroads.

Ladies and gentlemen, welcome, once again, to the Adrian Vowles Home for the Hurting here at the Tattersalls Club.

What a fitting climax to 1995 this do is, as 1995 without doubt has been the greatest rugby league year ever. It's a bold claim. But I hope in the few minutes of locking horns and getting the eyes down together that you will leave absolutely convinced, not by emotion of my bold claim, but by the facts that I will lay before you.

It's been a year so vast in its scope and implications for the code that even if we locked the doors of the Vowles right now, broke up into small discussion groups and talked nonstop until kick-off in the Prod on Sunday we would still only have time to cover one or two of the really big topics of season 1995.

1995 has been a year when tradition and vision have been at it hammer and tongs for the whole shebang. It's either been a slugfest or an arm wrestle, I can't decide which.

Let's go back to the start of the season. It all started so

3

swimmingly. Remember the fantastic opening weekend. Remember that fantastic celebration of League that was held just a couple of nights before the season's kick-off. Remember the big knees up in the Entertainment Centre. The launch of the wonderful, new-look, so very, very now, twenty-team competition. All the big names were there: Kerry, Arko, Quaylie, Bozo, Linda Evans, John Howard, Liz Taylor, Larry Fortensky, Kate Fischer, etc, etc, etc. The League linked the known world together and then produced that Golden Goose Yanni who came out with his forty-piece orchestra and told us all about His Dreams. Songs that meant so much to all rugby league supporters and players everywhere. Songs that told us that Yanni knew about the greatest game of all. That Yanni himself had experienced the thrill of scoring a four pointer. That he knew the pain of pulling a groin clean from the bone. That he had learnt from the shame of getting twelve weeks for going head high. I said to myself at the time, 'Yes, yes, yes. This is brilliant. The League has hit exactly the right note on the bed flute with this launch.'

he knew the pain of pulling a groin clean from the bone

Remember the first unforgettable weekend of the expanded competition. The mystery flight from hell that went from Sydney to Auckland, Auckland to Brisbane, Brisbane to Townsville, Townsville to Perth. And the red-eye from Perth to Sydney. What a weekend. A weekend in heaven with League mates and rugby league media.

Is it any wonder, after that fantastic opening heave, that some bigwig like Rupert Murdoch would say to himself, 'If there is that much fat, that much stupid, uncontrolled, hopelessly organised, rotting fat in the game, then there must be room in it for me'?

Is it any wonder when players who were being belted round the jaw for a few gorillas a week, smelt that fat on the fire, looked into the sky as the plane went over, and found themselves saying to each other, surely there must be a little bit more egg in this game for me?

THE STINK ESCAPES from the slacks

And so within weeks along the highway that is 1995 we come to the Big Split, the Long Goodbye, the Sad Farewell.

But face it, we lead humdrum lives. Year in, year out we follow the great clubs like the Rabbits, the Eels and the Bears. Clubs going nowhere, doing bugger-all. Days pass, weeks pass, years pass, seasons

4

pass without anything surprising happening. Then all of a sudden out of the box bobs 1995, and a code attempts to self-destruct before your eyes.

In years to come when we have kiddies and grandkiddies and they ask Dad, Mum, Grandad, Grandma, did anything interesting happen in your life, you will be able to turn around and with a grin from ear to ear say yes, yes, yes, kiddies. I was there in 1995.

I was there when the game clocked its first century. I was there when the game shot itself in the foot. I was there when Rupert rode into town shooting from both hips. I was there for the showdown at the Sydney Football Stadium between the young bucks Jamie Packer and Lachlan Murdoch when they put a stink on between the big sticks. It was a fearsome and terrible time, kiddies. Everyone cleared the streets. We stayed indoors for months. Only the brave and the bigger dared to go to games. There was no peace, only endless war. And it was all fabulous, stupid fun.

Sure, there was a lot of mewling about the problems from a lot of know-it-all types. Types like the Professor of League Roy Masters; the Tele Mirror's resident astrologer to the code Chippy Frilingos; the Police Royal Commission League Correspondent Ray Chesterton; super-mad Ray Hadley; Headmaster Ian Heads; Sherlock, the League's Super Snoop; Arold and Arfur,

a code attempts to self-destruct before your eyes

etc, etc. They were on the blub, all season, saying the jig is up. The League is cactus. We might as well get ferned and get down to Bondi Beach and pull a wave over our bonce and end it all.

But that approach is only for the gutless. You won't catch me climbing aboard the 380 bus with a one-way ticket. Because by the turn of the century 1995 will be considered the most exciting season ever. There will never, in our lifetime, be a better one.

THE PARROT'S PANCREAS points to the future

From March 1996 there will be two competitions going around in the toughest football competition in the world. I agree that even at this, the eleventh hour, there could be an outbreak of sanity and the smoking of the rugby league peace pipe. What worries me about this scenario is that no-one knows where the rugby league peace pipe is. No-one knows who was last seen with it. Some say Les Boyd had it last. Les swears he gave it to Scott Wilson. Scott Wilson says he left

we lead humdrum lives...

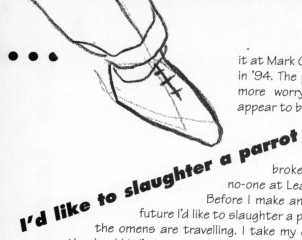

it at Mark Geyer's place after S.O.O. Two in '94. The pipe has gone awol. But even more worrying is that there doesn't appear to be any peace pipe tobacco left in the caddy at Phillip Street. And, sadly, the death knell of this UN-brokered peace plan is that no-one at League HQ has any matches.

Before I make any rash prediction about the future I'd like to slaughter a parrot and have a look at how the omens are travelling. I take my cue for my predictions from the dead bird's intestines. I do it in the Roman manner. The birds don't seem to mind. In fact, they're happy to help out. I always have a long hard geek at the entrails before launching my mouth towards a heart-felt stab at the future and when I did the bird this morning the signs were not good with regard to an outbreak of league peace today.

It looks as though we're stuck with the two comps, but the greatest game of all is ready for this. I believe there is room for even more rugby league competitions. I would love to see a third force come into the calculations.

There is, however, only one drawback with the two-comps scenario: how will we be able to tell them apart? When we stick on the TV next March for match of the round how will we know which comp we're watching?

Hopefully the codes will be distinguished by minor rule changes. The courts should legislate for one comp to drop scrums and re-jig the number of players down to, say, eleven. That would be a start. But it is merely cosmetic, fiddling at the margins. I'm looking for bigger differences. I want the ARL to declare today that it is the Smokers' League. More on this in a moment. The Vision Thing, the Super League, I want to be played in the nude. So with these two breathtakingly simple innovations we will be in no doubt about who is who and which is which come 1996.

Incidentally, if the Super League advertising can be believed—and I see no reason on the evidence so far to disbelieve it—next season should be a cracker from day one and we won't have any trouble telling which is which.

Any code that can put on the paddock week in, week out a bomb-laden bus banging into a 747 parked on the try line, or can promise the

I'd like to slaughter a parrot

thrill of watching a loon take the big drop from the black dot into a bucket of water, with a couple of bike tubes strapped round the cruets and a camera glued to the bonce, has got me begging for more.

Is it any wonder that television around the world is queuing up bellowing, 'Rupert, give us a bit of that!' And the good news is that Japanese TV will be on board the bomb-laden Super League bus from day one. They have already unearthed a Ray Warren, a Peter Sterling, a Fatty Vautin and a Steve Roach. This is tremendous news. The hard part for the Japanese TV boffins is translating terms like 'turn it up', 'promoting the ball', 'put away', 'bundled into touch', 'going the grope' and 'applying the squirrel' into Japanese so that they retain all their original meaning.

LOYALTY – 'What about me, Arko?'

Naturally, when talking of Super League I think of loyalty. Much has been made of the loyalty card throughout 1995. Let me state my own experience in that year so as there can be no confusion in the Vowles today. I was swayed early on by the Rupert Murdoch Super League Vision Thing. I was offered a playing package and signed on for $1.9 million, which I immediately took and cashed their cheque. Then I spoke with Ken Arthurson at a coaching clinic for the under-fours in Lithgow. I explained my problem and the ARL made a counter offer of $7.6 million to me to remain loyal. Which I took, so I understand the loyalty problem from both sides.

Now there was quite a stink kicked up recently when the news broke that million-dollar payouts were made to Bozo Fulton, Gus Gould and Mal Reilly for the hard yards loyalty-wise they had made this year. This caused a bit of a chat across the media about fairness, as there were others with their hands out legitimately.

I was in at Phillip Street last night helping Gus shovel the last of his million-dollar payout onto the tray of the ute. Arko put his head around the corner wondering what the noise was and I bellowed above the din, 'Ken, it's all very well these high flyers like Boz, Mal and Gus copping a wedge, but what about the ordinary league lover, don't they deserve a quid for remaining true to the tradition thing, man?' (That 'man' language is the sort of gear Arko understands.)

Ken screamed above the racket of the shovelling, 'You're right, H.G. Let me get back to you on that one.'

Ken got back to me this morning round about 4.30 with what I think is a very generous offer. Ladies and gentlemen, simply by being in the Vowles this morning you are all financial winners.

Arko and the ARL have devised a sliding scale which covers all possible categories of supporters of the code. Let's have a shufti at this sliding scale of payments.

For instance, if you have no interest in the League but hate Rupert Murdoch, you can collect $1,500 today from Phillip Street.

If you occasionally follow the League on TV, never go to a game and every so often run your eye over Roy Masters' column in the *Sydney Morning Herald* then you're in line for a $2,750 instant payout.

If you go to four matches a year and take more than two kiddies you can collect $5,670 each. And so on.

you're in line for a $2,750 instant payout

Now to the higher end of the ARL loyalty schedule of payments. If you're a coach and remained loyal, never mind the standard—you've hit the jackpot. For the emotional turmoil you've suffered in 1995 you will collect $1.23 million for each year of service to the code.

Ken has sent me along to the Vowles today with 1,250 official ARL loyalty claim forms. They are very detailed. There will be a category on the form that covers your interest in the game and your degree of loyalty. The forms are available at the back of the room. Can you each take one, fill it out, and return it to Phillip Street by no later than kick-off in season 1996?

Incidentally, if you know anyone else who has been loyal this year feel free to take a form on their behalf. But please, I hope no-one will go silly about this. The loyalty dividend is an honour system and I know that all of you will do the right thing by Phillip Street.

WHEN THE OFFAL hits the hotplate sweetness sizzles

The promotion of rugby league in 1995 has never been better. The game has reached new heights of recognition internationally speaking.

There is now enormous respect for Ken Arthurson and John Quayle and everything they have done for the code throughout the world, especially in Morocco and the old Soviet Union where the game is going gangbusters.

8

But who will sponsor the game in 1996, now that the prominent fitness-reducing-aid manufacturer's marvellous long-standing connection with the game has come to an end?

Despite the furphies put about by Phillip Street asserting that no-one is interested, I believe rugby league remains a hotly contested overripe plum atop the sports sponsorship tree just waiting to be plucked.

I know for a fact that the Canberra X-rated video industry is keen to get involved. They are mad about the League. The link would have been as natural as buggery as both trades feature fit young people doing what comes very, very easily. Phillip Street's thinking in rejecting the X-rated video sponsorship was that it may put some of the more traditional supporters of the game offside. I find that hard to believe knowing the League and the X-rated industry as I do. What better sponsor? After all, for the past decade we have had nothing but a cancer-maker as a sponsor. Isn't it time we did something a little more life-affirming for a change? And if the Tina Turner campaign taught us anything it was that the average Australian now thinks about the League just a little more often than he or she thinks about sex.

Sadly, this magnificent coupling isn't to be, because this morning at 11 at the Sydney Football Stadium, Ken Arthurson, on behalf of the ARL, will be announcing the new sponsors of the Rugby League for season 1996. Through me here in the Vowles he is extending an invitation to everyone to kick on to this important announcement that he assures me will be a milestone in the history of League.

You will be pleased to learn that Ken and the ARL have rejected a very attractive sponsorship package from the French nuclear industry. They wanted to sponsor the League with the slogan 'Let's Put the Bomb Back into Business'.

The French nuclear industry is looking to improve its image in the Pacific, and Phillip Street would love to get into bed with them soixante-neuf style. But this proposal was rejected on a very close five for—six against vote. An unnamed member of the board was asleep at the time the hands had to be put in the air, otherwise it would have been six-all and hence carried on the chairman's vote.

I am going to defy a Phillip Street embargo and surprise no-one when I say that in 1996 the Australian Rugby League will be sponsored by the Gauloise Cigarette Company of France. This bold sponsorship move gives the lie to those cruel claims that the code of rugby league is insensitive to events in the world around it.

soixante-neuf style...

9

I hear a muffled cry from the back of the Vowles: 'How will the ARL be able to get around government restrictions vis-à-vis tobacco sponsorship?' Well, in an absolute masterstroke Ken and the board have rewritten the rugby league rule book so that rule one now reads, 'All players will smoke while playing the game.'

With this single, dazzling, blindside piece of footwork the League has side-stepped the need for the Federal Government to be drawn back into the tricky tobacco sponsorship dispute. The League would not be telling the public what to do with the weed. The League would only be telling the players what to do. And since they have signed them all to loyalty contracts, who cares? It's so simple. It's so obvious. So Rugby League. For far too long the League has been making a monkey of itself by jumping through hoops just to please medicos and government departments who know nothing about making the hard yards and taking the big hits.

THE FIGHTS only start when the referee clocks on

And so quite logically we put the referees of 1995 on the slide and stab it under the microscope. 1995 was a year when the referee came of age. Referees finally took control of the code. I believe, as many of you do, that the game is ready for the forward pass. I believe that 'promoting the ball forward with the hand'—thanks very much, Ray Warren—will be seen as the greatest achievement of 1995. Now that we see it, week in, week out, it's so obvious. It looks good. It's novel. It's fun. It's football.

Elsewhere, referees have done away with the knock-on rule. The shepherd has been consigned to the ashcan of history. The offside rule has carked it, and good on the refs. Who can argue that we're not playing better league and getting bigger scores because of these simple breakthrough innovations?

referees finally took control of the code

Referees now believe that players should be able to bounce the ball down over the try line and get four points. Players should be able to score after they've run into touch. Referees have, at last, realised scrums are an even bigger joke. They now seem satisfied with a scrum so long as the Steeden sniffs the players' pants, any player's pants, on the way through.

I say hats off to referees for having the guts to change the game when all appeals to Phillip Street to modernise the code have failed.

Sure, it's easy to laugh. It's easy to bag. It's easy to say, 'What a joke! What a shemozzle!' Suddenly Barry Gomersall and Greg Hartley begin to look good.

And yet even in this great year of terrific refereeing innovation we still get whingers like Bozo Fulton who bag blokes for trying. The current crop of pea-pushers might not be very fit men and know bugger-all about the game, but they're trying. They take it a week at a time. What else can they do? What Bozo forgets is that they're blokes who are just trying to do their job.

Remember that lad, Phil Houston, who blew in from New Zealand to referee a couple of Tests mid-year in 1995? For years I have admired New Zealand rugby league and their marvellous attempts to come to grips with the modern policing of the game. With regards to this, look at Phil. I rest my case. There were times watching Phil in action when I thought the Grasshopper might have known something about the rules. What Bozo didn't realise is that Phil had never seen a rugby league match before he was given a couple of videos to watch on the plane on the way over from Auckland to have a blow in the second Test.

After his first exhibition Bozo bags him. Goes off! Calls him a goose, a dud, a joke, a has-been, a clown and a pillow. The world of league gasps. This, from the Australian coach! Pundits shake their heads. Bozo has gone too far this time. Boz will be up for a stiff fine for bringing the game, at the highest level, into disrepute. But not in 1995, he won't. That's the freedom that has been created this year.

All Boz has to do is apologise. Have a cup of coffee with the bloke. Try and explain a few of the more obvious rules of the caper and every-thing is ticketyboo. Final question from Fulton: 'Phil, now that you understand the philosophy behind the knock-on, how would you like to referee the next Test? Good. That's settled then.' Phil has a blow at Lang Park. Australia wins 46 to 10.

Other whingers like Gus Gould want to drag the team off midway through the second half, so impressed are they with the whistle work when Easts take on Manly. Is Phil worried? Not in 1995 he's not. When Gus is called in to Phillip Street to explain what the hell has been going on, the best Gus can blurt out is, 'Ken, John, Mick, QCs, lawyers, m'lud, it was a motivational ploy, honest Injun! I just wanted the team to win.' What a lame excuse. What's worse, Phillip Street believed this schoolboy howler!

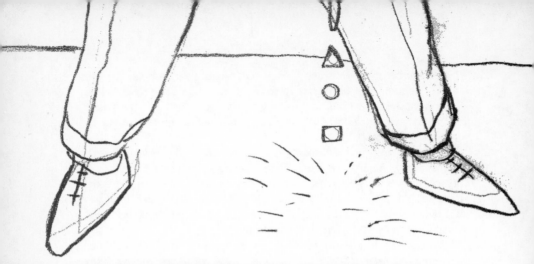

● ● ● ● **THE CLUB BUGGERY Player of the Year**

And so we arrive at that moment I look forward to every year when I announce on behalf of the judging panel the *Club Buggery* Player of the Year.

In 1995 there is, as always, a magnificent meat tray up for grabs. Today's prize is three hectares of mince.

The award is just a simple acknowledgement from everyone here in the Vowles; a way of saying thank you for what you have done for the code over the last twelve months.

In 1995 there has been a very rich field of quality runners. So much depth. It augurs well for the future of the game that there are so many great League lovers queuing up to snare the rowdy toot on offer.

In a packed field, first cab off the rank is the Norths stalwart, Tony Hearn, the Penalty Puller. We didn't see the best of the Penalty Puller in season 1995 due to a cruel and callous tribunal, but Tony put in a very bold claim wearing the maroon guernsey. He is the only player to be able to lay on a headbutt at State of Origin level and then pull the following penalty when the all-in broke out. A magnificent feat, Tony.

A very late entry is the St George Phantom Biter. I say good on you, Biter, for putting something back into the code that has been missing since your ex-coach Rocket Rod Reddy gave the game away.

Brad Fittler staked a bold claim as Player of the Year, not for his skill on the paddock or the fact that he is now recognised as the greatest player ever in the last five hundred years of the code's history—this must be true as Bozo keeps telling us all—but for his recent media appearances, especially his memorable *Footy Show* performances which had the normally unflappable host, Mister Teehee

Vautin, reaching for superlatives after Fatty regained his composure.

But even though all these players would have been worthy recipients of the 1995 *Club Buggery* Player of the Year meat tray, I believe there is a lot of daylight between this tightly bunched pack and this year's winner. This year's winner selects himself. My very good friends, it is with enormous pleasure that I announce that the *Club Buggery* Player of the Year is the Manly centre, Teasing Terry Hill.

Love him or hate him, thank goodness the code is big enough to have Terry in its ranks. Imagine the mayhem the world would have to endure if Terry couldn't find an outlet for his enthusiasm in the League.

What a season Teaser has had. Everything he has touched has turned to gold. His work with the kiddies in hospitals all over the world has been very widely regarded. His work with the legal fraternity, and the opportunities he has offered junior lawyers has been first class. His work with the nut and the headhighs against Illawarra and Newcastle speaks for itself. His tribunal appearances in 1995 broke new ground. They were a breath of fresh air and brought a little bit of old-fashioned show business back to Monday nights at Phillip Street. His marvellous appearances for the Blues in 1995 where he did everything to secure a NSW win. His work with the Sea Eagles newspaper

Tony put in a very bold claim wearing the maroon guernsey. He is the only player to be able to lay on a headbutt at State of Origin level and then pull the following penalty when the all-in broke out

where he writes a column aptly called 'The Other Side of the Hill' is out of this world. He offers his gag writer a chance to use some of his better gags. Very, very funny. Very, very consistent. Terry is prepared to be the back end of a cow if *The Footy Show* needs a live animal act to enliven proceedings. Teasing is always ready to have his picture snapped, which always shows the League in the most positive light.

In fact, everything he did this year screamed pick me, please, as the *Club Buggery* Player of the Year, and Terry, your efforts in 1995 have not gone unnoticed by the panel.

If there was a highlight that stood out from Terry's year above the rest, that highlight, which came very late, was the manpower v

A magnificent feat, Tony...

horsepower clash as part of the Wyong Cup festivities. It was Terry v Planned Magic, that marvellous Central Coast conveyance. I love these promotions where a horse is locked away in gate one, and toey Terry packs down in shute two. Both got away well when the starter sent them on their way. At the top of the straight I thought, by jiminee, the handicapper has got it dead right. Once the cutaway rail came into play, Terry went head high on the horse at the 200-metre pole and went away to score by a nose. It was a great run. It had 'be on me next time' written all over it.

Terry, your *Club Buggery* meat tray is available from Mario Fenech's World of Meats. Just present yourself at the back door of Mario's Marrickville Abattoirs outlet. And remember, Terry, at Mario's they put the beast to rest the way you like best.

IN CONCLUSION, the final nail in the coffin for 1995 is that I have been able to scrawl a page or two about this magnificent league year, the greatest year ever, and never once mention the State of Origin series.
THAT SINGLE FACT SAYS SO MUCH ABOUT RUGBY LEAGUE YEAR 1995.

ON THE DROP WITH THE DUCHESS

In this day and age, who isn't a big rap for Sarah Ferguson, the Duchess of York? A lot of well-informed know-it-alls thought she was merely a shopaholic cashed up with unlimited funds and not nearly enough things in the world to spend it on and it now turns out she can lose weight as well. What more does the future of the monarchy need?

ISN'T THE DUCHESS OF YORK, PRINCESS FERGIE, LOOKING A PICTURE these days? Her whole life has fallen into place and she is amazing the world every time the car door opens. Thousands of people are coming up to me at football grounds around the country screaming, 'H.G., what's Ferg's secret?'

Well, no big secret. A course of Roy Slaven's Slavenetics will work for you just as well as it's worked for the Duchess of York.

Roy flies over to the Palace every other week and maps new goals and incentives in Fergie's own personalised exercise and diet system. Slavenetics is a simple routine of exercise which deeply stetches the muscles with the minimum of movement and maximum of effort. The practitioner often goes into a deep trance-like state which does for the mind what the pressure on the muscles is doing for the body.

A Slavenetics workout always begins with the Power Pull. You simply place both hands around the neck, squeeze tight, then pull really hard for about thirty-five minutes. Nothing focuses the mind and makes the everyday problems of life fade into the background like the Power Pull.

The Pull is followed up, after a few moments' deep relaxation, by the Toe Tug, where you grab all five pinkies from small through to big on each foot and pull so hard that each one of them, quite literally, pops off in your hand.

Slavenetics also involves Stillson Therapy, a unique treatment only available at Roy's House of Beauty where Roy actually squeezes the fat away between the blunt jaws of the Stillson instrument.

Roy also recommends companion eating. This is the technique that keeps Madonna, Cher, Roxette, Kylie, Serena, La Toya and Dannii—to name a few—looking so good. The big man simply recommends when you're on the tooth to eat combinations of food. For instance, full-cream chocolate eclairs should always be eaten with sliced capsicum. Take a moment before slipping that tasty morsel of chocolate topping, puff pastry and fresh cream past the laughing gear to finely slice a whole capsicum and sprinkle it on top of the eclair. A piece of bread and dripping and Vegemite should always be eaten with coriander garnish. Pork chops should be loaded with basil and chives to take away the excess and unwanted calories.

With these correct combinations of food you actually shed weight while eating. Roy amazes clients down at the House of Beauty as they see the weight fall away with their own eyes while eating a plate of fish and chips followed up by a double helping of blackforest cake groaning under lashings of parsley.

 OF COURSE, IF YOU HAVE PROBLEMS PAYING FOR ANY OF ROY'S ANCIENT REMEDIES, EASTERN TREATMENTS OR FRIENDLY ADVICE, THEN YOU HAVE THE ONE BEAUTY PROBLEM ROY CAN'T FIX.

GARETH EVANS, arguably Asia's finest tele-visual mind, does his best work up north. Once the Big Foreign Affairs Beard breathes that tepid tropical air he can focus the mind and think outside of the circle that passes for criticism of the crystal bucket in our daily blatherings. The Foreign Minister blossomed mid-1994 when he gave ABC TV's THIS SPORTING LIFE a scrut from the safety of the Changa Langlands Bar in the Philippines.

WHAT A WELCOME RELIEF it is to know that with the Korean Peninsula about to erupt and shove the world into a nuclear abyss our Foreign Minister, Gareth Evans, the man who single-handedly knocked the Cambodian problem on the head, has had time this week to swan about in the fleshpots of Manila and talk television with arguably Asia's finest critical mind, the Philippines president, Fidel Ramos.

My late mail is that the big two knocked over the bilateral problems of trade, tax, immigration, customs, drug importation, regional security, youth suicide and defence in a couple of jiffs and had time to spare. They had a whip round on the international front, blitzed the ongoing Cambodian dilemma, made light of China's human rights brouhaha, sorted out Rwanda, talked tough to a couple of Russia's right-wing loons, cantered through the United Nations' funding problems, cacked themselves silly over

GARETH,
THE TROPICAL
TV CRITIC,
TARGETS OUR
INPUT INTO ASIA

East Timor, and breathed life into the old New World Order before a beautiful rag blade roister was dished up in a sticky date and mango sauce for lunch. After a feed there was still time for a man-to-man chinwag.

By this stage Fidel and Gareth had adjourned to the balcony to catch the breeze, with Gareth setting the pace, swanning about in standard-issue Asian kit: tie-dyed Pelaco shirt undone to the waist and the big pants wilting in the heat on the droop from the hips. He took up a spot near the flowering staghorn, lying back on the banana lounge with a large one handy and a man-size Salada and Kraft cheese single on the go.

Handlers from both nations declared television was the last item on the agenda and suddenly the two bigwigs struck gold. Three hours later they were still at it and loving it. They went through their favourite programs—MELROSE PLACE (is it really that wild?); NYPD BLUE (is it really that tough?); BAYWATCH (could any place on earth be more raunchy?)—and all of a sudden out of the blue up bobs ATV and THIS SPORTING LIFE.

Now for those who may have missed the program on its last go-round, THIS SPORTING LIFE simply featured a couple of boofheads camped behind a card table talking loudly at you, the audience, from the oblique angles of a darkened room. It was nothing to be scared of, just a thrash through issues of the week by the two hosts perched precariously on the sporting and cultural coalface of Australian life.

My co-host, Rampaging Roy Slaven, and I have always believed there was a screaming need for balance on a Monday night on the ABC. And we played our long suit offering what we do best, which is a long-winded spray about the burning issues that beset us all.

Mondays, for mine, have become unbearable, almost unwatchable on the ABC due to an invasion of comedy madness and hijinks. By the time you push through the 7:30 REPORT (which these days is all gags), then tackle FOUR CORNERS (now widely regarded as one of the funniest hoots on the crystal bucket) followed by Mister Mirth, Stewie Littlemore, and his ride through the issues from the tissues dubbed MEDIA WATCH, before you're knocked off your stool by the hard-core hilarity and unabashed slapstick of REVIEW and finish up with Mister Gags with the green pen, Kerrie O'Brien and LATELINE, you have every right to feel exhausted, to feel cheated and to scream, 'Enough!'

Roy and I felt there was need in this Monday night line-up for a program of fact, a program of record, a program of insight, a program of informed opinion. This is what *THE LIFE* offered. At no stage was there any attempt by the presenters or the guests to simply yok it up and play for laughs. We have always talked person to person, people to people, mate to mate, state to state across vast distances and across those even greater cultural divides which are seen throughout our near north.

But what of this fallacious charge that we sometimes 'send up' Asian leaders? Nothing could be further from the truth. It is true that from time to time Roy and I have made constructive criticisms of the way the leaders of some of our near neighbours conduct their business and their relations with us. But we have always asked for those leaders' approval before we have made any, repeat any, on-air comments, and they have always been in total agreement with what we've said. Furthermore, we have said nothing on air in *THE LIFE* that we haven't said to these leaders face to face.

It would be totally insulting to our great country and the ABC for Roy and myself to go on camera wearing funny wigs and skewy teeth, and doing funny accents with glasses akimbo claiming we were Benazir Bhutto, Kim Il Sung or Deng Xiaoping. That would be stupid and demeaning and we would quite rightly be ridiculed for doing so. We leave that to others who have the skills to pull it off.

In conclusion, what other current affairs program can claim to reach a potential audience of a couple of billion across Asia while rating bugger-all at home?

The only unfortunate aspect of this week's marvellous attempt to give our handiwork on The *LIFE* wider exposure is that the show is in recess and its future uncertain.

But Roy and I on behalf of the whole ATV crew thank Gareth for earning his money from our publicity payroll. It's only a pity he couldn't see his way clear to do the work when it mattered and when we wanted him to do it, ie, WHILE THE SHOW WAS STILL ON AIR!

22

Batman and Robin were the world's first great underpant superheroes. Years before Madonna began wearing the bra over the shirt, Batman and Robin pioneered the craft, pulling the fat Y-fronts over the skin-tight daks to hold up the floppy gusset and the droopy night tools. The inspiring fashion statement survived a thousand 'KAPOW!'s and 'HOLY TOLEDO!'s. Roy and I got this Dynamic Duo into a set of wheels. It remains a career highlight.

HOW A FROZEN FISH WAS BELTED, GIVEN WINGS AND TURNED LOOSE ON THE ROADS AS A BAT

Gotham City revheads and Bruce Wayne buffs, this time last year I got a phone call out of the blue round 11:30 one mid-winter's night. The moon was up and the dogs were on the howl. It was a call that was to change my life.

I was over the moon when I realised I was talking to Tim Burton, the director of the new-look, old-fashioned, pre-Robin *Batman* movie. I had him on the blower from his Palo Alto hideaway Stateside. Quite simply, he was ringing to ask the Slaven Nelson Group to design and build the Batmobile.

THE BRIEF - MAKE THE TROUSER STAY UP AND LOOK GOOD

The Batmobile order was a dream come true. The Group is no stranger to the big jobs but at that time our Lithgow-based production line was flat-out banging out the 1989 Slanel range. We halted the line and cleared the decks for Bataction.

My partner in crime, Rampaging Roy Slaven, the man they call the Australian Enzo Ferrari, downed his tools and assembled the Bat team out back in the shed. We sealed ourselves to secrecy, signing our names to the Batdeed in blood.

We threw on our thinking caps, fired up a cheroot, got a couple of large ones poured, locked horns and gave the specs T.B. had dictated by fax a squiz.

As nearly as we could tell from his hand-drawn notes and design suggestions faxed to our Lithgow HQ the new Batmobile was to be a quiet, unassuming set of wheels. The sort of unit that could follow a suspect through the Gotham City streets without pulling the head of every passing late mail specialist and track tout. These streets were so filled with evil that even young Robin was not allowed to be part of the crime-fighting team, though he was so desperately needed in the perennial fight against villains everywhere. Tim wanted—or at least our interpretation of his scribble suggested he wanted—something tasty with European lines and a smooth ride that would not shake the camera off its mounts.

THE BEAST TAKES SHAPE

With this our main objective, we got to work knocking up a design buck that same night to get a feel for the Batbeast.

24

The new Batmobile was to be a quiet, unassuming set of wheels. The sort of unit that could follow a suspect through the Gotham City streets without pulling the head off every passing late mail specialist and track tout

truck -skull

Straightaway Roy set about pushing the design envelope inside out. The only thing we could find out in the shed to model up the buck with was a dozen frozen mullet that Roy had stashed in the freezer. The mullet, side on, with a couple of whacks from the cold chisel, became the basic elevation of the Batmobile.

THE THEORY

I need to outline a little of the group's philosophy concerning the car design caper. There have been many magic moments in automotive design in the last fifty years. Look back over the card yourself, take time to give history a good hard geek.

There was the fullblown genius of the Ford Edsel, the controlled inspiration of the Nissan Cedric, and the eye to the future that informed the creation of the Leyland P76.

Roy and myself decided to overlook these highpoints and follow our own gut feeling about crime, police work and the whole Batman story.

In throwing together the box and dice, the first cab from the rank was the '62 Valiant. The fins at the rear make a bold, horizontal statement as well as reminding you where the spare is every time you look at the boot. ●

We scarcely ate, sleeping at the benches. One night we collapsed with exhaustion and, as the sun rose the following morning six months after we began our quest, it dawned on us that WE HAD IT.

Up front at the business end the B-team settled on a touch of the Tucker. The pointy end in the Batmobile is a tribute to that great individualist—as well as providing a convenient place for that extra spare when you seek a bit of off-road action. These two design motifs form an axis over which the rest of the unit is draped. Roy and I never made any secret of our admiration for the Mod motor scooters that cruised Britain in the mid-sixties and occasionally bob up in Fine Young Cannibals film clips of today. These are a deadset inspiration to any designer.

I know I have spoken elsewhere about my lifelong affection for Enzo Ferrari. He said to me just before he died: 'H.G., I wish I had the courage to just keep adding mirrors, lights and knick-knacks until the Vespa or Lambretta grinds to a halt under its own weight. Just imagine a fire-engine red Dino with fifty-seven headlamps on board.' I just nodded knowingly as Enzo passed away. The man was working and creating to the very end.

BACK TO THE BEAST

Once we had fashioned the mullet buck we did extensive testing in the methane-driven wind tunnel rigged up in a shed next door to the Lithgow abattoirs. On into the night, week after week, we fiddled with the buck, the wind tunnels and the drawing board, looking for the right mix of elements, with Roy driving us until the team dropped.

We scarcely ate, sleeping at the benches.

One night we collapsed with exhaustion and, as the sun rose the following morning six months after we began our quest, it dawned on us that we had it.

The Batmobile was there melting in our hands. We threw the prototype into the freezer.

The final tunnel tests proved our suspicions. **WE WERE LOOKING AT THE 1989 BATMOBILE.**

We rushed the buck from the Lithgow wind tunnels to the Dutch flotation labs that told Benny Lexcen in '83 he was on the right track when he burst through the doors with the winged keel tucked under his arm, shouting, 'Hey blokes, have a squizz at this and tell me if it will float!'

The tank tests, using the coloured dyes, showed that we had stumbled across a deadset inversion of the normal state of affairs with the Batmobile prototype. The tests proved conclusively that the car could travel at greater speeds in reverse than forward—a secret feature that gives Batman the edge in tight situations where the unusual is called for. After all, surprise is the only element that keeps Mr B. ahead of the Joker, the Riddler,

the Penguin and the dreaded Mr Freeze.

THE WORK BEGINS

The B-team was able to make the step from model mullet buck to full-scale fabrication. Originally Roy and I had

27

car-skull with ox-tongue

conceived the whole unit as no bigger than a Mini Minor or a Fiat 500. But the film-makers were not able to see Batman in a Mini. This was the only time the producers interfered. And I take my hat off to them for that freedom.

Tim Burton, Michael Keaton and Jack Nicholson all spoke to us about getting some length into the beast. We took this on board as a serious request from the artistic coalface. What could I say about my vision? They were paying the bills.

THE CHASSIS – START WHERE THE RUBBER MEETS THE ROAD

We began at the bottom with the chassis. We were stuck, we didn't know where to turn. And then we stumbled on a Leyland P76 Targa Florio that just happened to be sitting out in front of the works, left there by the disgruntled Slaven Nelson Group's accountant. This gave us the length we needed. We stretched it with an extension of 7.6 metres. The body of the Batmobile is built up from styled Slaven Plank and aerodynamically finished off with heat treatment to smooth away the joins.

To get the required width we laminated the plank in a vertical and horizontal mosaic and stuck it together with a new super glue, Dinko Lukinitis.

THE DONK – THE BRUTAL 9 BREATHES LIFE

The Batmobile was looking a picture but the real battle had just begun.

'What about the donk?' Roy panted one morning as we pushed the beast up onto the jack to have a go at the tail-light wiring. By this stage the Batmobile was getting so heavy that we needed to work a power pack up from scratch.

Ralph Sarich had offered the project a 16-valve orbital outboard for the beast but somehow the aesthetic line of the design was broken with a couple of big bulges up back. We wanted a nice line that allowed the flow of air to pin the monster to the road. Nissan offered a V12 prototype that was going to be dropped into the '91 EXA. Toyota rang to insist we use a very new piece of gear from its HiAce dragster that powered the HiAce to the World Van Titles in Sacramento last year. We were not satisfied that any of these could deliver.

We settled on Roy's Brutal 9, a brand new turbine-driven prototype. This power pack has been well documented in the car mags. A brilliant piece of lateral thinking from the House of Slaven.

● ● ● ●

CAR-BONE WITH OX-TONGUE

The car tooled up with The 9 belongs in the six-second club and when you approach the ton you feel as though you are crashing through the sound barrier, which is a very nice touch. But the principle is quite simple: the fuel mixture is exploded in conventional cylinders in the ceramic, liquid-cooled engine block and then through the manifold ducting. The hot gas is forced into a turbine located alongside each wheel. The air rushes through the blades of the turbine and directly drives thirty-four-inch wheels. The Brutal 9 gives the Batmobile phenomenal poke over the critical first two hundred metres.

The 9 will run on any sort of fuel—two stroke, unleaded, diesel, super, Avgas, lard, solid paraffin mix, Space Shuttle, liquid hydrogen, Fruity Lexia, and olive oil. The curious thing is no matter what fuel is tipped into the tank, economy remains the same point five of a kilometre per litre.

The gearing is simple viscous coupling, but in retrospect the power-to-weight ratio is all wrong, accentuating the hardtop's tendency to understeer.

POLISH – THE DEVIL IS IN THE DETAILING

Once we had all these central ingredients in place and were confident enough we had the stab to pull the skin off the custard, we were able to satisfy Bruce Wayne's personal touches. Batman wanted leather slip seats to prevent the cape from catching in those quick get-aways. Bruce suggested a higher roof-line on the hot rod so that the canopy didn't knock his ears off when the air ram slammed the lid of the widowmaker shut.

Movie fans, this is a pre-Robin bag of tricks. There is no room for that cute talk from Dick. As soon as the Caped Crusader slips into the conveyance, having slid down the Batpole—'Atomic Batteries to power; turbines to speed; ready to move out'—the Brutal 9 sparks into life and off she shoots on the prowl for evil.

That is the history of the car that graces our screens. When you see the movie try to recall the work of a couple of young Aussie battlers who made their dreams a reality with the Batmobile.

THE BOAST

We feel that our work is on a par with the creation of Interscan, the over-the-horizon radar, the solar telephone, Benny's winged keel, the fork and the electric brick.

When will the local industry be able to take the Batmobile on board? The Slaven Nelson Group is banging out proto-type model number three and is hoping to put the beast into production in limited numbers to take on Brockie at Bathurst and Professor Prost at the Melbourne Grand Prix in 1997.

A BLOKE ON THE BRIDGE OF A BARGE
with a Blunt Biro and a Bunch of Dates

• •

The Adelaide Arts Festival has always set the pace artistically for the nation. As the runners turn for home and head up and salute the judge, you find the Big Blow-Off in Adelaide blouses the opposition on the line by a short half head in a good year by the length of the straight in a dud.

32

● ● ● ● ● ● ADELAIDE, THE FISH CAPITAL OF ASIA!

Wherever you have a shufti around South Australia these days there is a renaissance of activity happening right across the state. Poke about and lift the doona and you will find South Australians going in hard, early and often. They are having fun and winning while they're at it. The whole place is abuzz with excitement. The doom and gloom of the State Bank financial fiasco years have long departed on the Overland Express. The happy ute full of fish days are here again.

This was brought home to me last night as I spent a very exciting evening fishing for gar off the Brighton Jetty.

Incidentally, have you had a chance to get down there and have a geek at what the builders and architects of South Australia plan to hurl into St Vincent's Gulf? It's fabulous. It is a jetty with the lot, a much better structure than that thing which is laughingly called a jetty currently parked at Glenelg but waiting for the next high tide to drag it down the gulf past the tip of Kangaroo Island never to be seen again.

I hadn't planned a big night, a full-on fish frenzy, but knowing that I would be in town for a motivational spray, I whipped up a foursome to ● ● ●

she's just mad about fishing and killing things with a big hook

● ● ● ● ● ● ● ● ● ● ● ● ●

join me on the planks of the Jetty for a gar kill.

Adriana Xenides came along. Rex Hunt blew in—and doesn't he love SA fish!—and making up the numbers was international superstar and Adelaide Festival patron Paula Yates. She loves Australia and Adelaide in particular and is just mad about fishing and killing things with a big hook.

I got there at 10 pm, got the lines set by 10.30 and spent seven happy hours chewing the fat, talking Adelaide and pulling in big fish.

With four of us on the tug we quickly filled the back of my SA-made Mitsubishi Pajero and had to resort to giving good, big fish away to the early swimmers who began bobbing down for a bomb or two off the top deck of the jetty at first light before they went to work. I *hate* giving good fish away.

We pulled up stumps at 7.30 am all agreeing that the night was the happiest night we had spent in years and planning to meet on the jetty on 1 March 1996 to see the Adelaide Festival off in the most meaningful manner.

All the chat last night was of this renaissance happening across South Australia and of South Australians forging a future when none had boldly been doing so before. Paula Yates was very impressed with the incredible activity. She said it reminded her of Michael Hutchence on a good night. Her words were, 'It starts so early, and keeps going for so long and so loudly that I often have to resort to wearing ear muffs.' She was offering an international perspective sure, but I could only nod in total agreement.

THE FACTS SCREAM SO LOUDLY IT HURTS

My very good friends, if you don't believe me just draw your co-ordinates through the following events and handiwork from top local names and achievements.

The South Australian rabbit virus is the talk of the world scientific community. Just how did it escape from Wardang Island?

34

Just how good is this calicivirus? How many rabbits will it kill when it really gets going? These are questions that now sadly will probably never be answered.

(In passing, why have the shooters of this state let the community down in such a gross and uncaring way? You would think with so many people on the bang recreationally speaking that the rabbit population would be well under control and that the humble bunny could, by now, be number one on the endangered species list!)

South Australian Water recently went up against drops from all over the nation. At the death, all the talk was not of the nation's winners. (Who can remember them?) All the chat was of the nation's duds. A litre of brown from Mount Barker came in last. And there was an awful lot of daylight between the rest of the field and the Mount Barker syrup.

Everyone at the '1995 Water-Off' wanted to know just how bad the Mount Barker gear was. What did it taste like? Could you actually keep it down if you hurled it past the larynx? So many questions, so few answers.

Incidentally, Dean Brown and John Olsen are on an absolute winner with this proposed state Water sell-off. Is it any wonder that business identities around the world are queuing up to get their mitts on the South Australian water supply, and the Mount Barker beige in particular?

And isn't Brown the perfect name for a water salesman in SA?

On the sporting field there has been nothing but success for South Australia and South Australians. Players from this state are packing down in the engine room of the finest AFL side this nation has seen in a generation. Tim May has brought the crazy world of cricket to a shuddering stop with his yet-to-be-disproved allegations about wristy subcontinental cricket capers with the purse. Port Power are setting the pace in football jumper design around

could you actually keep it down if you hurled it past the larynx?

• • • • • • • • • • • • • • • • •

35

Asia. The Adelaide Oval is still the prettiest cricket ground in the world and if I read the smoke rising from the burnt-out circle of bullet-ridden wagons that was once the Australian Rugby League, the Adelaide Oval is soon to be home of arguably the best rugby league side this nation has ever seen.

There are travel delights awaiting every tourist who steps off the plane at the airport or out of a bus or train. Their scope is staggering. People forget that the Victor Harbor Bluff is still here. Many international visitors think that the Bluff went to Victoria on the back seat of Sam Newman's Porsche when he nicked the Adelaide Grand Prix. But the Bluff is still here and I believe it is getting bigger. So is the Big Lobster at Robe and the Big Parrot out at Kimba. They are all screaming out in unison to the traveller jaded by what the world has to offer, 'See me! See me!'

The whole joint is going off. And the icing on this renaissance cake is the new SA number plate proposal, 'All the Way with SA'. Hasn't that got a ring to it? It says it all. What a perfect backdrop all this activity makes to the 1996 Adelaide Arts Festival.

Is it any wonder that so many top international artistes, who could have done almost anything, anywhere in the world next March, have been lured to pack the lunch box and the skimpy gear and head to the City of Churches in 1996?

STABBING WINNERS IN THE ARTS, IT'S NO JOKE!

Look, I know what it's like to get a festival card together in a town that is so buttoned on artistically speaking as Adelaide is. It is an absolute nightmare. Roy described it once as 'sliding down a two-kilometre-long razor-sharp banister using the night tools as the only means of deceleration'. That just about nails it.

There are so many people with opinions who want to put an oar in. There are so many big ideas, and when you're on the bridge with your hands on the wheel you have to take them all on board. What's more, these days there is so much experience locally, not only of the Australian and Asian stage, but of the world stage, that it makes it

sliding down a two-kilometre-long razor-sharp banister using the night tools as the only means of deceleration
● ● ● ● ● ● ● ● ● ● ● ● ● ● ● ● ● ●

harder to steer your choices through the witch's hats that make up the giant slalom of the Arts Festival selection process.

It's not as easy as it looks. When Roy and I were heading up the Lithgow 'Days of the Dates' Festival selection committee throughout the eighties (a decade which saw 'the Dates' widely acknowledged as the must-see multicultural event on the East Coast of Australia), we always saw our challenge as one of breathing new life into the gusset area of the community's trousers so that the wedding tackle chimed in with a chorus of high Cs of approval. It is a very neat trick if you can pull it off.

For Roy and myself the Festival program was a fiendish Chinese mystery box and expanding ring puzzle where the first piece into the frame is also the last. You can't play one without playing the lot. The trick, we found, was to hold the whole solution in your mind before you begin bumping the pieces into each other on the board in front of the public's gaze.

The Adelaide Festival director Barrie Kosky has taken on board our total card approach in setting out the marks to hit in 1996. I have admired his work from a very careful distance for years now. No-one can open up a booking sheet and stab at it with a blunt pencil quite like Barrie. If you're making a map of where to go he is the one you want at the wheel of the showboat. He is prepared to slash and burn and let the artist's blood spill where it may. Internationally in the caper he is known as 'the Velvet Squeeze'. When they speak of his skill, it is always in very hushed tones.

For the last few months the Squeeze has been out back in the Festival shed packing down at the whiteboard coalface with a bunch of

she'll walk out at centre stage as nude as her recent Playboy appearance

dates and a lot of big names. The sniffs from under the B & D Roll-A-Door suggested that the captain was brewing up something very big.

And now that the program is through the rinse cycle of the Hoovermatic and the Festival souvenir tea towels are pegged out on the Hills Hoist to dry, what a doozey it turns out to be! This Festival treasure map has poke where it hurts, grunt up the back where it matters and that little bit of crazy, in-your-face, Bay Tram, trousers-round-the-ankles magic that will have people from around Australia . . . no, as you were . . . that will have people from around Asia screaming 'Adelaide 1996!', long after the tents, the bunting and the bed flutes have been packed away.

NANCE – THE MASTERSTROKE THAT HAS THEM ALL SCREAMING 'YES!'

The genius of the blueprint for next year's clambake, the key piece of the puzzle, was the inking of Nancy Sinatra. Nancy is the peg that enabled all the other pieces to fall into place. It must have been a day of sheer adrenalin excitement when the fax in the Festival office said, 'Yes, Baz, Nancy is on her way!'

I have been a big rap for Nance for years. A lot of know-it-all critics have bagged Ms Sinatra for being in poor voice over the last decade, much in the way they found Joan Sutherland's throat suspect just before she retired in August 1990. (Just a few short weeks before Collingwood broke their thirty-two-year hoodoo and won the 1990 AFL Flag.)

I deny that Nance's pipes are on the blink. She can still cut it. Whenever she pops into Roy's for a full-on, old-fashioned karaoke night she is always in fantastic voice. She can do the lot: opera, Gregorian chant, barber shop quartet on her tod doing all four parts, three-tenors work, metal, house, techno, thrash, hip hop, national anthems, choral at Easter, power pop, golden oldies, country. She performs blue.

Can cut it cabaret-style. Does the hits. Light opera, G and S, is a doddle. At a pinch she will open the Mary Poppins song book.

She is very, very versatile. Her duets wth Malcolm McLaren next March will be talked about whenever people gather on the banks of the Torrens and talk about what a bloody great boat Popeye is!

At the end of the night when you're exhausted by her sheer artistry she'll walk out at centre stage as nude as her recent *Playboy* appearance and lay a couple of those really big hits on you, like 'These Boots Were Made For Walking' and 'Something Stupid'. You'll think that you've died and gone to festival heaven!

By signing Nancy Sinatra, Adelaide, you have the drop on the opposition and have made other Australian festival heads green with envy. But face it, these big interstate shindigs are run by pillows and show-pony duds who wouldn't know class if it squeezed their blackheads.

Everywhere you peek at this comic there are highlights. Malcolm McLaren is ripe and ready to drop from the tree. *The Blue Hour* is a cheesy must-see with a touch of the lewd that will have you begging for more while howling at the moon with delight. *Excavation* has blown me away more than once. I was rubble for days the first time I saw the Batsheva Dance Company strip off and go the grope, while the Bauls of Bengal turned me to cactus one night in Bombay. It lasted a month and you know, I don't think I have fully recovered.

But without doubt the strawberry sitting smack dab in the middle ● ● ●

DORK - BONE

No-one bashes the timbal quite like Tito. The way he hits the drum, he could be running a workshop in home-slaughtering

• • • • • • • • • • • • • • • • • • •

of the icing on top of the cream on this very attractively baked three-layer-high sponge is the luring to Adelaide of the great Tito Puente. I am a Latin buff. I love the sweet sounds of the samba, which huffs and puffs to me of one thing only—the language of love. The samba is the muffled sound of the trousers hitting the carefully polished floorboards under the mirror ball, with the bright red, off-the-shoulder sequined frock slinking over the hips aided by gravity alone. No-one bashes the timbal quite like Tito. The way he hits the drum, he could be running a workshop in home-slaughtering.

WHINGERS AND WIND FARMERS CAN ALWAYS FIND SOMETHING TO WHINE ABOUT

In this rocket-fuelled atmosphere of sheer excitement we have to pause and acknowledge that in this day and age, when arts dollars mean votes, you have to put a lot of store in what the members of the community think and how forcefully they express their artistic opinions. Experts in the arts are flushed out whenever a festival flag is run up the pole and people are asked to stand to attention and salute. And so we come quite rightly to the comments of those in the know about this 1996 Festival program.

Big Bob Francis went on record not long after the Festival flag hit the pole saying in the *Adelaide Advertiser* that he is not 'an arty-farty sort of person', but he believes the 1996 stink will be the best Festival ever. When he says he is not 'arty-farty' he doesn't mean this literally, as he popped out more silent-but-deadly trouser coughs and body temperature air scones than probably anyone else on the planet this century.

Bob described Barrie's blueprint of the Festival as 'the best ever'.

40

His exact words rumbled, 'I have never, ever been to a Festival performance. But the 1996 Festival is the best yet.' That's an enormous leg-up from a man who obviously knows his art and knows what he likes. Next March Bob is going to break a life-long pattern of abstinence from Festival do's as he plans to go to see the Batsheva Dance Company.

What a tremendous feather in Barrie's cap knowing that Bob is on his way and going to the Batsheva. When this news hits Anzac Parade tickets will be scarce. I just hope there's a venue big enough for the Batsheva Bob rush. No, bugger it, the Festival owes Bob for this one. Nothing in the previous Festival programs for the last thirty-plus years has ever got him out of the house and now the Batsheva will. Surely the Festival must give him a ticket to every performance. When Roy and I were working 'The Days of the Dates' in Lithgow we knew you couldn't buy publicity like that.

The Lord Mayor, Henry Ninio, burst out of the Town Hall in the mayoral robes screaming, 'This is a well-balanced program which also celebrates the city of Adelaide. There is something about the geography of Adelaide that Melbourne and Sydney cannot match.'

No, I haven't a clue what he means, either.

The Lord Mayor started well and then he buggered it up by stating the bleeding obvious. He could have been misquoted or his text edited to make him appear an idiot—this can happen from time to time in the ● ● ●

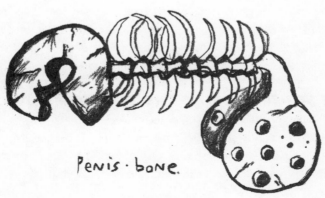

Penis · bone.

41

a work of raw desire, uncontrolled jealousy, seduction and up-close table-dancing that lifts the skirt completely

● ● ● ● ● ● ● ● ● ● ● ● ● ● ● ●

Murdoch press. But I find it very difficult to believe that a paper with a worldwide reputation like the Tiser, a paper that employs Leo Schlink and publishes the Campbell Column, could harbour a cell on the local government desk who wants to see the current incumbent out of the Town Hall fancy dress.

The chairwoman of the Independent Arts Foundation, Jessica Dames, said, 'The whole city is going to know there is a festival going on. It will lift the state out of the doldrums.' I knew the arts had some poke locally but this is tremendous news. I know the people of Eyre Peninsula will be jumping up and down come March knowing that the dreaded doldrums will be consigned to the ashcan of history.

The only dissenting opinion I have flushed out of the daily blatherings has been the very loud voice of very, very successful AFL football coach Graham Cornes. As soon as the program saw the light of day Graham was on the phone to me and on the bag. Cornesy ripped in. 'The whole show, H.G., is far too expensive, with zero mainstream appeal, thereby ignoring seven-eighths of the population.' Cornesy is a man with an intimate knowledge of popular arts in Australia, but he may have overlooked the fact that we have football to keep seven-eighths of the population interested in life 67% of the time.

However, I note that Cornesy has said, 'I quote Barrie as saying that one of the Festival highlights, Operation: Orfeo, is like watching a painting that sings, but I wonder whether it will be more like watching paint dry!' His words, not mine. Very, very funny, Graham, as usual.

THE SQUEEZE OMITS THE BLEEDING OBVIOUS

I cannot fault Captain Barrie's Festival charts, except that I know for a fact that 'the Giant of the G Chord', Ian Turpie, is available at least two days in March, on the 7th and 19th. I cannot fathom how a man of his artistry and skill has been overlooked yet again by the Festival.

42

The omission is an act of obscene cultural vandalism and for mine borders on criminal negligence. Would calling for a royal commission be out of order?

As the *LA Times* was moved to say when Turps appeared for three sell-out shows at the Hollywood Bowl last February, 'To see Mr Turpie swan his way through "Running Bear" bum-on is to realise why song has become the dominant musical form.' If Captain Baz moves quickly and cracks open one of those hollow Lithgow Bank sponsorship logs, Turps could be piped aboard the Festival barge in time for the jump. And don't tell me the South Australian public and Geeza Cornes wouldn't stand as one and salute.

My second criticism is this: why hasn't Roy Slaven's erotic opera *The Laid Carpet is Still Warm* been given a guernsey in 1996? This work documents in three unforgettable acts the struggle of a young lad from the Riverland who, after blowing into Adelaide in a desperate bid to find happiness, packs down in front of the big sticks with the Adelaide Crows. He can take a grab. He can get the hard ones on the turn. He can get them out front or coming from behind.

The Carpet is a work of raw desire, uncontrolled jealousy, seduction and up-close table-dancing that lifts the skirt completely on the dog-eat-dog world of AFL football at the highest level. This wicked rip-snorter has already seen record-breaking performances at La Scala ● ● ● ●

and Covent Garden. In a tribute to the Adelaide Festival Roy has specifically redesigned *The Warm Carpet* to be performed in the Gepps Cross Abattoir, but not while it's shut down, at weekends or when it's dark at night. *The Carpet* can now be performed as the author intended, ie, while the abattoir is in full operating mode and the slaughtering of live animals is actually taking place on stage before our very eyes. What a marvellous backdrop the live kill meat motif would be to this work!

But, above all, it is a piece that could pull the 1996 Festival ensemble together as a whole. Imagine the casting possibilities. Malcolm McLaren, donning the fat shorts and the Camry Crows footy jumper, would bring a fresh, lively read to the central part of Tony, the kid who didn't know if he wanted to play footy or go surfing. Malcolm could handle the tricky upper register gear in a doddle.

Nancy Sinatra selects herself to play the pivotal role of Liz Taylor, the woman that Tony left behind. Liz's aria that opens Act Two, set in a Riverland orchard while she picks oranges, still tugs at my heart-strings and makes me goosey all over every time I hear it.

And don't tell me that Annie Sprinkle couldn't bring the tricky part of Adriana, the girl from Port Wakefield with the lot, to life in the most convincing manner.

The Batsheva outfit and the Whirling Dervishes would make a most impressive chorus representing both sides of the football process, ie, the two teams.

Oh no, this is a glaring omission from the Festival card, and it is even harder to fathom given that *The Carpet* is a piece that screams to all South Australians about that unfulfilled quest for AFL success.

But apart from these oversights, congratulations, Adelaide. You have a deadset winner on your hands if you can leave it alone long enough to enjoy it.

Since I was asked to have a munch on it by the *Advertiser* I haven't changed my opinion of this year's spree one iota. This 1996 blueprint is a fat cracker shoved right in the back door of the arts experience of Australia in the nineties.

44

The Adelaide Festival has plunged it in. Lit the wick. The bunger is timed to go bang on 1 March. Hats off, Festival! Pants off, Captain Barrie! Hurl open the gates at the Patawalonga boat haven, I'm bringing the zodiac inflatable in for the whole shebang.

Fossilized dick-bone in gravel-pit

LICKING THE LIPS:

The Luge......

It's only a matter of time before Australia bashes off the lip and bags gold in the luge. If this great sport was promoted correctly Australia would produce home-grown gold medallists in time for the next Winter Olympics. But we need to get real and put aside a budget allocation of, say, $3.4 billion per annum to get the slippery ice caper up and running in all states. Until then the rest of the world will laugh at us and quite rightly consider us the sick jokes of the winter sporting card.

THE LUGE – LIE DOWN AND LOVE IT

I spent a couple of crazy weeks hanging around Barcelona during the Olympic Games with that great continental sporting identity, Prince Albert of Monaco. The Prince is a funny bloke, very, very blue. During one fabulous night the Prince, Brigitte Bardot, Katarina Witt and I made up a foursome dancing the night away at the Games Village Disco. As dawn broke the Prince let his pants down just a little and told me exclusively that Sydney had a rich fruit and prune cheese platter with the 2000 Games now in the bag. Albert wanted me to thank the Sydney Bid Committee for what he called 'their kind consideration' and said that he had 'always wanted a sky-blue 1968 fully restored E type Jaguar'. The Prince certainly gave me plenty to chew over on the long flight home.

My friends, as the games of the 26th Olympiad slip like a chock-a-block-full Gladbag over the rim into the wheelie bin, it is time that Australia takes a well-polished size twelve Clark's desert boot to the Olympic movement and persuades them to give us the Winter Games in 2000 as well. Imagine superathletes of all persuasions making a beeline for our slopes. This

47

would be just the fillip winter sports downunder need.

I mount this Winter Olympic bid with a very personal motive in mind. Ladies and gentlemen, I love the luge. I am obsessed by slipping down a firm but well-greased shute in the attractive skin-tight gear that leaves nothing to the imagination.

I will never forget—what a formative image it was—when as a kiddie I copped a peek of Darrell 'Huge' Eastlake crouched luge-trackside at the 1968 Winter Olympics clad only in the bright pink and dayglo green chicken and sprinkler patterned 100% Mambo ockanuis. Huge was on the burst, baring the knees to the forty-seven below, with a wind chill factor of seventy-three, going in hard early, explaining the mysteries, the art, the magic of the greatest sport ever invented, the luge.

It was one of those rare moments in life when the future was let in.

When I look back from the vantage point of 1996, I don't know what made me take up the sport. In Nuriootpa, where I grew up, there was no snow, no luge tracks, no luge coaches, no books in the library and no luge literature (eg, *The Brain and the Luge, 101 Ways to Luge* or *Luging for the Beginner*) explaining how to get a start in the caper. In fact, there was a conspiracy of silence when it came to the sport.

I was handicapped loving the luge in the Barossa Valley but I said, 'Bugger it, bugger it, there has to be a way.' Anyone with the vision, the desire, the guts and the gameplan can over-come lack of facilities and ideal conditions. One night not long after seeing Huge in action I woke up clutching at air, bathed in a cold sweat of stupidity once again at not seeing the bleeding obvious. You didn't need snow or approved Olympic standard frozen runs to go street luging

48

and what better way to prepare for an Olympics where it was certain any kiddie with a bit of drive from the backline would wear green and gold.

NO SNOW SHOULDN'T MEAN NO SHOW

The next morning I was drawn as if by a steel hauser to the top of Bulli Pass on the south coast of NSW.

I didn't have a bucket, nor a luge sled.

I had none of the fancy gear, the skin-tight suits, a CSIRO-designed stack hat in Kevlar, or a motivated spray before each run from Norwegian supercoach and 1972 Olympic medallist, Oofy Smith-Smythe. All I had was a sheet of corrugated cardboard and a home-made skateboard using old pram wheels and axles from trucks. But if I was going to represent Australia I wasn't going to powder and pillow for the want of a bit of Olympic-endorsed gear with five boofheaded multicoloured rings plastered all over it. I was a lugist with attitude. I was going to show the world just one ring, a winning ring, a brown ring.

At the top of Bulli Pass there was a moment of truth. I threw away the cardboard. I clambered onto my sled, back door to the bitumen.

I let go of the anchors. I gave it a poke. I tore off centimetres above the asphalt. I killed it. One run and I was bitten by the bug.

What is it about the luge?

It's the fear, the raw stomach-churning, gut-spewing, retching fear of plunging into a jet black hole with no light at the end of the tunnel and the most likely outcome DEATH. That's why I like it. That's what all lugists like.

CHAMPIONS DO IT EVEN WHEN THEY'RE DEAD

I am often asked at luge clinics by kiddies and youngsters of all ● ● ● ●

49

ages what the drawbacks are to other Australians clambering onto a luge slops shovel and giving it a crack. Well, none that I can see. There is crashing or flopping it out, as it's known in the caper. Taking a flop on a luge spoon is like hitting the side of the shopping centre head first, lying on the bonnet of a V8 Commodore HSV Senator using the three kilometres of surrounding car park as a run-up. In the luge everyone takes the carpet, rolls in the brown, plays the back door trumpet at some time or other. There is nothing to be ashamed of if you go over the lip.

The most important thing after a big luge flop-out is to get back on the spoon and give that killer run a good, hard, swift boot up the date.

The first time I came off the rickshaw was at Bulli Pass. I broke a wrist. I pulped a fibia. My groin was pulled clean from the bone. I punctured a lung. I was shredded with cuts that needed 127 stitches and had six broken ribs. But even though I was gaga, I knew if I cooled off I would never mount the board again. That desire to ride sorts the wheat from the chaff. Anybody can do it once: you just hang on and survive. But the champions do it even when they're dead.

My worst accident was doing 'the Bone' at Victor Harbor. The Bone is a vicious straight drop, perfect for psychopaths who don't give a fig or an offal stanger about tomorrow, and arguably the first and only street luge run in the southern hemisphere. The first day I did the Bone, the drop was shrouded in fog and mist. A dank onshore wind howled in from the southern ocean whipping up around fifty knots at the summit of The Bluff where the Bone begins. I took off unsighted. I lost control on the first corner. I began wobbling up over the track lip. I bought it, stiffing out on the part the locals call 'the Axminster Vortex'. The board shot out from underneath me killing a jersey cow

50

that was foolishly grazing nearby and smashing into a thousand pieces. I was, now, doing the Bone on my back, snookfaced and green. On the Double Hairpin I was spewed out over the lip. I landed on my face outside the track and slid the next 3.7 kilometres to the base of the Bone face-down unconscious . . . It was a miracle I survived.

I spent the next six months in intensive care with the Bone thing gnawing away at my brain. It was giving me nightmares even in the middle of the day. The doctors diagnosed it as Bone fever. The only way they kept me horizontal in the cot was a fifty-fifty pethidine and morphine drip straight into the central cortex of the brain. Seven and a half months later, I was released from traction. The next day, against my doctor's advice, I discharged myself from the Royal Adelaide hospital. I superglued my busted luge bucket back together. I hitched to Victor. I scratched and clawed my way to the top of The Bluff. I took a deep breath. I heard above the howling southerly the familiar strains of Angry Anderson singing the Sydney 2000 Olympic song 'Brown for Glory' and launched myself down that terrible descent. I did the Bone again. And this time I thrashed the Bone. It was the greatest moment of my life.

But this is all in the past. This is the story of just one lugist who proved it can be done. With the Winter Olympics coming in the year 2000, plus sponsorship and lamington drives and the selling of five million bumper stickers screaming 'THINK LUGE and LAUGH', I make this bold claim that Australia can grab gold from the drug-fuelled Germans, the intellectual Swiss, the grunting Canadians, and the supercharged Thais in a sport that should quite rightly, by the turn of the century, be our own.

Weed Woodis On the Spot In the Stewards' Shelter Shed After the Third

I love going behind the closed doors of any sport and having a squizz at how officials go about regulating their code. I love to see the beaks of sport disciplining their wayward and more excitable customers. Racing is no stranger to controversy but there is bugger-all basis, in fact, for the suggestion that the caper is crooked, as this hidden camera report from the front line indicates.

● ●

WEED FAILS ON THE JOB

Racing and the spring carnival, I love it all. Pulling on the fashions, going the plonk, getting on the tooth at the back door of a Roller, seeing people go crazy and broke, copping late mail from those in the know, queuing up in the payout line as soon as they jump, seeing bludging horses belted, getting aroused as they swing for home, having a tipple with a bunch of losers while grinning inside and, above all, going home a winner. It's all tremendous fun and worth every penny of the effort and expense.

This year the greatest thrill I had on course was sitting in with the stewards helping them with their enquiries into the running of every race throughout the four-day carnival at Flemington. I was allowed to view proceedings as a representative of the horse owners and breeders of Australia.

I was simply staggered by the professionalism of the whole show. Nothing persuaded me more that racing is in excellent hands than when the young Lithgow hoop, Weed 'Der-brain' Woodis, was asked to step into the stewards' room and explain after an appalling ride aboard On the Job in the third on Oaks Day for that magnificent ● ● ● ●

Bungalow skull

trophy, the Thorsteen Slaven Cutglass Sherry Decanter. This race honours the memory of Roy Slaven's great-great-grandfather, the first person to realise that the public of Australia would come in droves to the races when they could be confident of seeing a first-class display of hoops hitting horses.

Let me state right from the top that I am, as part-owner of On the Job, the first to admit that the horse is not an easy ride. 'The Date', as the stable has always affectionately called the conveyance, is a temperamental brute of a horse just one shade shy of killer. He is a bay chestnut by Rooting King out of Princess Pants Off, a lineage that gives speed to burn in the first thousand metres plus a dyed-in-the-wool staying finish. The horse can let his aggression out over any distance between 1,200 and 2,400 metres. We had set him for the Cutglass for months and while his trackwork had been a bit peaky, well, you have to be in it to win it.

On the Job came into the 1992 Decanter line-up a 40/1 pop, but found plenty of admirers on course in the ring, and a specking of support from a wide range of touts and wind farmers on the TAB.

Now I agree with many of the racing press that it was wrong to hurl a five kilo-claiming boy onto the Date, a boy who, incidentally, was having his first city ride. Hindsight is a marvellous gift but for mine the kid put in an absolute shocker and deserved all he got.

THE CASE AGAINST THE KID IS CONVINCING

Woodis was asked to step into the stewards' room straight off the scales after the ride. He arrived still wearing the silks of puce and lime with little flecks of carrot tumbling down the front. He looked like a condemned man who had just given his last breakfast back to the jailers.

The room went suddenly quiet when Weed stepped in. The VRC club secretary, Sir Ernie Sigley, asked Weed to leave it alone for the next few minutes adding that there would be time enough for a fiddle when the hearing was over. Weed was asked to come to attention and stand on the spot.

The chief steward, Julio Iglesias Esq., turned on the bright light and shone the beam straight into Weed's eyes, totally blinding the youngster. This softening-up procedure went on for the best part of three hours. There wasn't a murmur from the vast crowd on hand.

Then there was a flurry of activity as the hearing got under way. Prosecuting for the VRC was Warren 'the Croc' Negus, a very big legal noise trackside from the top-flight turf firm of Dittman, Gauci, Moses and Mayfield-Smith. Weed's jaw hit the floor when the Croc made his entrance. The kid realised any hope he had was gone. All the boy could do was throw himself on the mercy of the court of enquiry.

Head beak for the club, Baby John Burgess, entered the stewards' room in purple and pink robes and a gorgeous red fright wig clamped down up top. He banged his gavel and got proceedings under way. The charges were read. Half an hour later the club's main charge was revealed. Weed had failed to let On the Job run on its merits and had failed to ride the horse out.

WEED WILTS WITHOUT A WHIMPER

The Croc was unleashed to make the prosecution's case. Warren came out swinging, giving the youngster both barrels, pleading with the stewards to make an example of Weed, and begging that the maximum penalty of death be handed down from the bench. The big man smelt an easy kill. He flared his nostrils. He circled the defenceless child. Shuffling his notes he moved in, ● ● ● ●

pounced, and quite literally tore the hapless blubbering kiddie limb from limb on the spot where he stood. The so-called quiet man of racing addressed the hoop with a chilling spray that I still recall with horror when I wake round midnight in an ice-cold sweat kicking myself for failing to back horse number seven in the third.

The Croc pulled the lips back and with a bagful of courtroom tricks he learnt from Perry Mason bared his foul and rotting teeth and began.

You could hardly miss Vic. He was the big gent dragging a dead 5.7-kilometre white pointer behind him

'Woodis, you are a joke. Woodis, you are a farce. Woodis, you need to go into the room of mirrors, and have a good hard look at yourself. What have you got to say, boyo?'

Without pausing for a moment the Croc bore on. 'Weed, the video evidence of the running of the Decanter shows you loaded On the Job backwards into the barrier gate at the start of the race. Der-brain, you did not make a murmur of protest as the starter, shark hunter Vic Hislop, climbed the stand. You could hardly miss Vic, Weed. He was the big gent dragging a dead 5.7-kilometre white pointer behind him as he mounted the club's aluminium ladder. Even when Vic reached for the button and shouted, "Ready, steady, go!", you sat there oblivious to the fact that you were facing the wrong bloody way. When Vic let them go—correct me if I am wrong, Woodis—you appeared to be casually munching on a pie which you pulled still warm from your slacks moments earlier.'

At this point Weed attempted to offer an explanation, saying that he hadn't eaten anything since the previous Tuesday in a desperate bid to make the weight. But the Croc was having none of it and he pressed on. 'Weed, when you get the Date finally going forward, the rest of the field has passed the 1,200-metre pole. At the point of the turn you go wide, Shane Dye-style, no doubt looking for the firmer going on a track that most ratings experts had assessed earlier in the day as faster than glass.

'Do you get my drift, Weed, or am I going too fast?' bellowed the

Croc. 'Having got out into the members' car park on the horse you then make a beeline for the judge straight past your relatives and fiancée who are having a sausage sizzle trackside opposite the 800-metre pole. Once again—correct me if I'm wrong, sonny jim—the video shows you stop the conveyance in mid-stride, scoop up a beautiful, rare, recently slaughtered T-bone in club colours (plus all the trimmings from the salad bar) and while you sink molars into the luscious meal you take time out to sign a few autographs for your sister's kiddies. Now, Weed, while I'm sure the VRC committee would encourage and applaud your efforts, it seems to me, to put it blunt-ly, that during the running of a race is precisely the wrong moment to be doing your bit of public relations for the club.

'Finally, when you realise after a lengthy chat with your future father-in-law that there is still a race to be run and won, am I correct in the surmise that you try to illicit a run from the Date by dan-gling a Mars Bar from your whip in front of the horse's nose? And don't tell me I'm draw-ing a long bow, Woodis, because it's all there in black and white on the video. The fact that the horse flew home for a fast

And don't tell me I'm drawing a long bow, Woodis, because it's all there in black and white on the video • • •

BUNGALOW-SKULL with STEAMING MONKEY BRAIN

finishing, "be-on-me-next-time" ninth in a field of seven seems to have more to do with the natural ability of On the Job rather than your efforts at so-called riding. With a little more vigour, Weed, I believe, the committee believes, the *Age* newspaper's racing panel believes, the Wizard believes, and the world believes that the Date could have won the Decanter in a doddle.

'I rest my case and hope the bench finds you convicted as charged but I, one Warren "the Croc" Negus, leave you, Weed "Der-brain" Woodis, with the following questions. Have you been taught how to hit a horse? Have you been taught that the harder you hit them the more likely they are to win? Have you been taught that it is up to the jockey to hit them and not members of the public you pass in the running?'

Sensing a pause in the big man's tirade Weed attempted to say something by way of defence. But the Croc was not done yet. He walked up to the kid, grabbed his throat and lifted the lad up to his eye level. All that the little Weed could see was a tomato-raw face, blood-shot eyes, and teeth which spat flecks of foam all over his dial whenever the Croc said anything.

'Weed, did the trainer Mungo "Chooka" Willessee tell you to give the horse an easy run? Did Chooka in fact tell you to run the horse dead? Were you aware, Weed, that the owners had gone the plonk on the sta-blemate Kylie's Wonderbra, which, surprise, surprise, won the race? Were you also aware, Weed, that On the Job returned a positive swab after the run?'

Here the Croc paused briefly while he referred to some hastily-written notes in legalese. 'Returned a positive swab to the following drugs: cocaine, Valium, elephant juice and to use the vernacular of the street, M'Lud,' and here he tugged a forelock in the direction of His Honour Baby John Burgess, 'uppers, caffeine, downers, reds, acid, blues, eccie, ludes, aspirin, plutonium, blood and bone, mogs, smack, M and Ms, grass, speed, horse, poppers, rhino horn and red-hot go fast.'

The Croc dropped Weed to emphasise his point. The boy was nothing more than a limp wrung-out rag, exhausted by the Croc's searing indictment of his chosen craft.

At this stage I made my excuses to the chairman. After all, there is only so much random, gratuitous, legal violence a grown man can take. I slipped away for a comforting thirty or so, secure in the knowledge that justice was being done and that the racetracks of Australia are completely safe from incompetence and unprofessional conduct.

THIS NATION LEADS THE WORLD IN LEISURE PURSUITS. WHEREVER YOU LOOK PEOPLE ARE ON THE BLUDGE, LOLLING ABOUT ON THE BANANA LOUNGE WITH THE FEET UP. EXERCISE IS THE LAST THING ON THE MENU. WITH STRESS ON THE RISE AROUND THE WORLD IT IS ABOUT TIME WE BEGAN EXPORTING THESE SKILLS. WE CAN PUT OUR EXTENSIVE EXPERTISE AT DOING NOTHING TO GOOD USE EARNING THOSE HARD-TO-GET EXPORT DOLLARS.

The Big Drop
With the Bike Tubes Round the Ankles

HOLIDAY MAKERS, at this time of year Australia gets a few moments to down the flint-hard tool that has been boring non-stop into the employment coalface for the past twelve months, twenty-four hours a day, seven days a week, and for a couple of idle moments we can think of nothing but pleasure and heaps of it.

In case you've been too busy to notice, long gone are the days when the only form of holiday pleasure was a loose-hipped rhumba across the slate-tiled patio at sunset, past the white, sun-damaged plastic furniture to the alfresco, steel tray-mobile groaning with bite-sized Saladas, individually wrapped Kraft Singles, little green pickled cucumbers and slices of imported super-strength pepperoni attractively displayed as conversation starters. Gone are the days when you simply got Uncle Theo and a bunch of mates who you only saw once a year round for a night of munching and making small talk clad in big print, flower-patterned muu-muus and hipster straight legs while the pig on the spit turned to perfection above a tray of red-hot heat beads.

All that hoo-ha has been consigned to the toxic, green-blue algae and radioactive ooze. Even so, many of us still find it hard to let go of the vice-like grip on the tool and unwind. Many of us cannot let pleasure have its belial head and allow it to weave its wicked and relaxing magic.

I love pleasure and there are so many ways to get it. After all, we are living in the nineties. When I want to let it all hang out I get down to a secret love nook on the South Coast I have affectionately called 'Dunscreamingatheref'. It's not much of a shack, just a couple of rooms whipped up out of Hardieplank and a deck large enough to fillet a fish on and fire up a Weber.

After a couple of hours of pressing the pedal to the metal extra hard in the ute to get there, I slip the car into neutral and hide the V8 away from the stickybeaks under the weeping willows on the river bank. No-one knows I'm there. The trouser area is the first thing to relax and when I get out onto the deck the only sounds are the sounds of serenity. There's the lap of the water, the lonesome call of the cormorant and the quiet clang of the strides hitting the floor.

I slip the buttocks down firmly onto the banana lounge, reach for a can of peeled grapes, hurl a couple past the larynx and let the rest of the world scream along the tollway of life to an uncertain oblivion.

At Dunscreaming there is always a tight line with a snook or flathead on the tug. And you can while away hours, days, weeks just fiddling about doing bugger-all.

But when it comes to the pleasure caper a lot of people are too busy to think for themselves. When you have gone past caring then it's time to see the sensuous specialists at the Slaven Nelson Leisure Group. The Group believes it has on tap the finest pleasure possibilities available in Asia today.

Oh sure, make the comparison if you must! Take the nine-day package holiday to Angkor Wat, have a shufti at the Royal River Hotel in Bangkok, waste a fortune rafting the total length of the Grand Canyon, go troppo on Dunk, bag a mullet from the Brighton Jetty, and be amazed at the size of the Big Banana. But when you have sated your appetite and there still remains a nasty, unsatisfied taste in your mouth ring the experts at Slaven Nelson Leisure. We can look after your total pleasure needs.

For starters, no matter where you're going you'll get better with Slanel Air. It's the airline that puts the pleasure back into paying. Total gratification begins as soon as you step on board a Slanel service.

Take our Mudgee to Eucla red eye service, the Fisherman's Special. This is the only airline service in the world that allows you to wet a line and bag a fish while actually in flight. Don't worry if you forget the bait and the tackle in the rush to get away. Both are included in the cost of the fare. Once you have pulled a fish still flapping fresh from the ocean below, you immediately think of cooking it. No problem. Slanel Air is the only carrier in the world to offer on every flight in first, business and economy classes an all-wood barbeque service with thirteen choices of wood on board from Radiata Pine through to exotic table quality Thai teak.

In some flights we have even ripped out two rows of seats and added vast holding pens and tanks of fresh and salt water so that you, the traveller, can have your selection of fish, fowl, crab, game or cattle killed as you like before your very eyes, before seeing that same selection thrown onto our hotplate and cooked to perfection by our specially trained staff.

Slanel realised early on that people only go to sleep on planes because there is bugger-all to do.

Our all-nude flights across Australia from Port Hedland to Lameroo have become the talk of the travel world. These are famous because three times a week Bernard King and Keith Floyd make themselves available to run nude cooking classes.

Many of my business associates from the football industry find there is no better way to relax after a couple of days making the hard yards at the international conference coalface than climbing aboard the Lameroo nude express with Bernard King showing you the more attractive side of his kitchen tools.

● ● ● ●

63

Slanel's 3.30 pm daily Nude Twister flight out of Nuriootpa has never flown without every seat fully booked and a recent geek at the bookings sheets shows the earliest Twister seat Slanel has available is on 23 July 1999.

If you're taking Slanel for in-flight luxurious-ness, then what better way to start your pleasure than by making a trousers-off week at Nude Island your first stop?

On Nude you can do everything: pig shooting, volley ball, python wrestling; you can play football with Kevin Sheedy; be tackled by the Brick with Eyes just for fun; talk to Paul Sironen about why the Poms hate him so much; or take the big-drop bungee jump over and over again. The bungee jump is very popular. After a simple three-hour climb up the scaffold our experts tie the bike tubes round the ankles. You take the plunge. As you come through the clouds you get a total image of Nude spread out several kilometres below. Just as you think you'll hit the turf the bike tubes come into their own and you pull up laughing, screaming, 'Move over, pillows, it's my turn next!'

At sunset Nude comes into its own. When the sun goes down on that tropical paradise and the wind rustles the palm trees round the lagoon, the night's activities begin in earnest. The house band, dressed only in their instruments with plastic fruit in their hair, loosen you up with a reggae-funk groove of Supernaut's 'I Like It Both Ways'.

Magic is the only world that truly captures what Nude has to offer. From the time you wrap the laughing gear round the first of the evening's long ones, with the crazy, multicoloured brollies poking out the top, to the time the hired help comes round and tips you back in your chair, opens your mouth, sticks the funnel down the gap and shovels in the after-dinner mints, you'll know you've never had it so good and that, yes, total self-indulgence can be had at an affordable price.

It is our personal commitment to service and your obvious satis-faction that has made Nude the envy of every other island on the Queensland coast.

By the way, if you're coming to Nude this holiday break leave your hangups in the Slanel Gold Pass Transit Lounge on the way in. Because on Nude Island, nude means fun.

Incidentally, the most often heard comment at the departure lounge—as happy holiday hoons return to civilisation to begin what can only be loosely termed the rest of their life—is the simple but so satisfying, 'On Nude, I have never felt so free.'

My very good friends, when it comes to pleasure why be limited by what your own tired mind and jaded palate can cough up? Get a wriggle on and quiz the Slaven Nelson Leisure Group about possibilities you have only dreamed of. Be amazed that we thought of it all even before you did.

PLEASURE – IT'S ALL UP TO YOU. HAVE A THINK. HAVE A QUICK LIE DOWN. BUT TAKE A TIP: YOU WOULD BE IDIOTS TO YOURSELVES IF YOU DID ANYTHING ELSE BUT RING AND ASK FOR OUR BOY AT THE BACK OF THE PLANE, LEON.

GOING THE GROPE

GETTING THE
HARD ONES ON
THE TURN WITHOUT
BEING PINGED
FOR HOLDING THE
BALL · · · · · · · · · · · · · ·

In the ABC debate caper there was always a natural sympathy for the side Andrew Denton was opening the bowling for. He is so wristy, so hard to put away, with so much sheer pace off the short run. He proved the winning edge when two evenly matched sides packed down over the topic that football is stupid. When push came to shove and the audience was the umpire, our side emerged convincing winners when the Applause-o-meter did its thing.

WINNING, IT'S THE ONLY THING!

Ladies and gentlemen, let's be quite clear about one thing right from the top of this spray. I have come here tonight with only one purpose in mind. I have come for your votes.

As you can already see from the pathetic offerings thrown up by our opponents, our side of the debate here in the cauldron of the State Theatre represents everything that is good, healthy, positive, progressive and right about the Australian way of life. To state the bleeding obvious, our side of the debate is the side of truth.

Our side represents the right of all us Asians perched down here on the Pacific Rim to attend the match of our choice, at the code of our choice, on any Saturday or Sunday we choose. To simply go to fixtures where we can let the hair down. Go a little bit crazy. Support a team. Eat a pie at half-time. Stand under a brolly and have a beer. When our team wins it's off to the local Thai take-away with the whole family in tow. And if we lose because of the mad mongrel in the middle with the whistle then we go home for a good old mope and a day or two of feeling very sorry for ourselves.

Tonight, my very good friends, we have put aside party political differences. We have to drop the petty squabbles about which team is best, about which code is best, about who was the greatest, about which game was the greatest of them all. We have to unite not only for our sake, but for our children's sake, and for the Australian way. We have to join together as one, united by our love of the game, and see off this desperate and pathetic bid by our opponents to argue the case that football is stupid.

My colleagues and I represent the side of the true believers. We are carrying the torch tonight, lighting the way for the people who can see that bright shining light on the hill.

We are here on a mission, a mission that will end only when the central referee Campbell McComas gets up at the end of hostilities and asks you here in the State Theatre to judge our efforts in the time-honoured tradition of banging your hands together.

Make no mistake, ladies and gentlemen, this is a night loaded with historical import. With our Prime Minister, the well-known Collingwood and Canterbury-Bankstown supporter, making the hard yards with the Yanks in Washington before flying on to London to go the grope on the Queen once again, we here tonight in this place, along with the Western

Australian Green senators, are running the country. We are setting the co-ordinates for the twenty-first century and beyond.

So seriously did our side feel about our task that we wrote a pact together out back in our blood. The rusty nail that we found in a loose floorboard was sterilised between dips as we wrote the pact, taking it in turns to supply the ink from our own veins.

Winning this debate for us, ladies and gentlemen, is not a matter of life and death. It's far more serious than that.

Before I begin let me introduce my fellow team members who have their shoulders to the wheel for the Australian way tonight.

Kicking with the breeze in the second quarter in the number two jumper is Laurie Lawrence, a man who once described one of his swimmers as 'tough as bird poo on the car roof'. Laurie was obviously talking about himself.

Laurie isn't here to talk about the caper from some lofty artistic closet or from a preconceived hopeless joke of an academic point of view. Laurie was a footballer. He has played the game at the highest level. My very good friends, Laurie has pulled on the big shorts. He has pulled on the boots. He has felt the arousal when he pulled on the jumper. He has hit it with a cold spoon and run on and played eighty gut-wrenching minutes. And at the end of the game all Laurie asked for was a place to bleed and a dog to lick his wounds.

Laurie only gave the game away because he was sick and tired of making the great Ken Catchpole look good. He still has all the skills; in fact, I believe he still has a season left in him. He looks fit, he is fit. I have had a fiddle and a look at the X-rays and there is nothing wrong with Laurie. He still has speed to burn out wide and can score from anywhere on the paddock. When Laurie talks he uses the voice of experience. He is here to point up the poorosity of the opposition's case and to demonstrate from his own love of the game that they haven't a clue, not a bloody clue, what they're talking about.

Finally, when we run with the breeze again in the last quarter, we ● ● ● ●

are lucky enough to have Andrew Denton, arguably Asia's finest football mind, guarding the back door in the number three jumper.

Andrew Denton, ladies and gentlemen, is not an ornament to the game. Ladies and gentlemen, Andrew Denton is a monument to humanity. Football is the winner for his involvement. Sure, it's easy to say that. But this man's love of the game is so great that he has chucked in a leisurely life of comfort and security at the ABC and hurled himself headlong into the maelstrom that is Channel 7, the greatest football network in the world. Forget the drivel you read in the daily papers about what the big A is up to at Seven. Andrew has been snapped up by 7 to do only one thing, and that thing is to head up their football team.

WHERE ARE WE GOING?

Now, from the top of our dig, we on the side of GOOD in this debate need to set the tone. We need to open a road map of where we're going because our opponents in their opening spit simply failed to do so.

So to football. The world needs no further discussion other than to say that we in Australia play the game at the highest level in several codes. In rugby union, rugby league and AFL we lead the world. In the world game, soccer, we're on the way up.

'Stupid' appears to be the bone of contention here tonight. I went to the *Macquarie Dictionary* and found that 'stupid' has four possible meanings. The Macca Book of Words describes 'stupidity' as:

A. LACKING ORDINARY ACTIVITY AND KEENNESS OF MIND;

B. CHARACTERISED BY, INDICATIVE OF, OR PROCEEDING FROM MENTAL DULLNESS;

C. TEDIOUSLY DULL AND UNINTERESTING;

D. IN A STATE OF STUPOR.

My very good friends, many things in life are obviously stupid. We don't dispute this. Take competitive swimming. Now *there* is a stupid activity.

Everyone agrees that getting up very early

in the morning, braving the cold in midwinter, diving into the deep end, swimming up and down following a black line on the bottom, wasting the best years of your life, urged on by an over-enthusiastic coach on some mindless quest of Pan Pac gold or Commonwealth Games selection is obviously stupid.

And I know Laurie agrees with me on this one.

In a similar category with swimming are ironing, watching *Neighbours*, Zsa Zsa Gabor's ideas on fashion, underwater hockey, *The Home Show*, the Talking Beard and pig shooting. They are all 110 per cent stupid. No argument from us!

But compare them to football and I think I can rest my case. There are stupid things but football isn't one of them.

Ladies and gentlemen, football is a metaphor for life. It sustains life through the long winter months. It keeps you going every day of the week for the twenty-two home and away matches and the four weeks of finals.

The football week begins with Friday night, Saturday afternoon and Sunday matches.

Post-hooter time is taken up with clocking the television coverage and re-living the highlights.

Monday it's all post-mortems. Taking in the reports in the daily papers. Scanning the radio for club news. Going to the TAB to collect the winnings on the Pick-the-margins and Pick-the-scores. Adjusting the ladder positions at work and in the lounge-room at home. Waiting for the tribunal decisions to come through and the video citings to be announced.

Tuesday, there's the injury lists and going to training.

Wednesday is the night off where you can relax or begin planning for end-of-season activities after September. At your leisure you can calculate the odds for the home fixtures and begin making your selections and filing your tips.

Thursday, more training and the vital team selections.

71

Friday, the anticipation is just too much. Then Saturday and Sunday come and it all begins again.

As you can see, football offers a total week of involvement.

People enjoy football because it enables them to do what the great gurus and spiritual leaders say is the trick of life itself. Football forces us to live in the present. For a couple of hours while your team goes round the troubles of the week are forgotten. The dodgy muffler can fall off the car but it can wait to be fixed. The leaves can remain in the gutter. The bank manager can rot in hell—at least until the final siren. Adriana Xenides could appear nude on *Wheel of Fortune* and no-one would give a bugger while the match is still in progress.

What else in life offers such certainty, such fulfilment, such satis-faction? Name one other human pursuit that can take you from cradle to grave which is so completely environmentally friendly.

To paraphrase the greats, to tire of football is to tire of life and if that were to happen we may as well call for the vet and the elephant gun to end it all.

THE UNSPOKEN MYSTERY OF THE PIGSKIN

Whatever aspect of life we look at we see football offering us some-thing. Let me focus on two aspects of life and compare them with football. They are religion and art.

In religion, if we're going to make a case with the cardinals in Rome for Mary MacKillop to be canonised then surely, football lovers, we should submit the names of rugby league administrator Ken Arthurson and the former Carlton great Bruce Doull. Now I am all for Mary getting the big honour, but St Arko the Patron Saint of Bludging on the Blind Side and St Bruce the Patron Saint of Flying Doormats have a pretty attractive ring to them as well.

In the arts I defy our opponents to come up with a more powerful, moving or erotic image from the whole world of art than a big pack of fit blokes in club colours, flying at centre half-forward in a grand final with a minute to go and five points difference in the score at the MCG on the last Saturday in September.

I defy them to produce an image that has more raw beauty and joyful artistry than a rugby league scrum. The scrum has it all. Let me take you through it. The referee indicates the penalty. The front rowers lock arms with their opponents and at the back big men bend over, part the buttocks and shove the head up, while the little man feeds this twelve-backed monster and the game gets underway again. Now *that* is art.

These two images do more for this nation than Rembrandt's *The Nightwatch* did for the Dutch, than Michelangelo's *David* did for Florence, or than the billions of entombed warriors did for China.

But I don't want to stop there. I want to tender two artworks in evidence tonight. Firstly, this magnificent snap of a Canterbury-Bankstown Bulldog in action.

For those who can't see as well as they'd like this is the Squirrel-gripper Martin Bella on the bellow looking an absolute winner with the electrical tape and bandage wrapped round the head busting them up the middle, standing in a tackle, looking for the supports about to unload. The football-bereft Renaissance failed to produce an image like this.

I raise the case of the Squirrel-

73

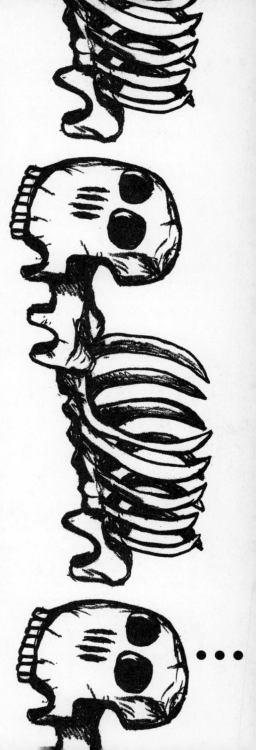

gripper because the ancient Greeks strove for a well-rounded complete being. The ideal was someone who could give their best on the playing arena on the weekend and then be back up on Monday packing down with a positive contribution to society in another area of human endeavour. The Squirrel-gripper, Martin Bella, is such a man. On the weekend he is as tough as teak, a ball-playing prop. During the week he makes the hard yards in the surgery hands-on in the healing caper.

I ask you to imagine a world without football, a world where people like Martin with his skills have no way of releasing the pent-up pressures that life in the surgery force upon them. Just imagine the sort of loonies that would be on the loose then.

THE FOOTBALL IS OUT OF THE BAG

Ladies and gentlemen, I now move to my second exhibit. Take a long hard geek at this fabulous, fabulous object. For those up the back I am holding up an AFL football made by our greatest sculptor, T.W. Sherrin. Henry Moore, eat your heart out! Look at the colour, the shape. Feel its texture! I know the great European sculptor Brancusi gave the game away when he clapped eyes on the work of T.W. Sherrin.

No matter how hard the greats worked they never got an object looking as beautiful as an unkicked footy. You can have fifty Tom Roberts paintings and thousands of Jeffrey Smarts and they won't add up to a fraction of what this ball means to the people of this nation. I challenge our opponents to produce another artwork equal to this.

Finally, ladies and gentlemen, when I look out into this vast auditorium here in the State Theatre I don't see anybody looking stupid. Behaving stupidly. Doing stupid things.

I don't see anyone in front of me suffering from mental dullness.

I look to my colleagues on the side of truth in this fixture and I see no-one stupid there. No-one lacking ordinary activity and keenness of mind.

I swing my gaze past Campbell McComas. It goes without saying that Campbell isn't stupid. Campbell is a deadset genius.

However, there are three people here tonight in a stupor. They are our opponents. If you want to see stupidity seek it there and not in football.

Ladies and gentlemen, in forty minutes' time Campbell will get you to play your part in the proceedings when he asks you to judge our efforts.

Firstly, pat yourselves on the back for coming. Pat yourselves for making the effort, having the vision, the guts, the gameplan to get down here tonight. Pat yourselves on the back for spotting the only three loons on the loose in a stupor here in the State Theatre tonight. See them as a bunch of hapless water buffaloes. Put them out of their misery. In that scenario, my very dear friends, tonight you are the safari with the elephant gun. Don't let yourselves down. Don't shirk the load when Campbell asks you for an effort. Hurl your hands together for our side of the question. Hurl your hands together for the Australian way. Hurl your hands together for the future of the nation and reject totally, convincingly and completely the pathetic assertion that football is stupid.

My very good friends, experience the thrill of being on a winning team, for once in your life. When the big bloke gets you to clap, add a little icing on the cake by imagining that you are at the MCG along with another hundred thousand football fans on that one Saturday in September, and regardless of who you support simply let yourself go tonight, here in the State Theatre, and support us when you clap by shouting, loudly,

Carn the Blues!!!

DAVID BOON

As the Scottish Laird, MACBETH

When Boonie bagged an AFI award for Best Actor at the stink in Melbourne last year, I took my hat off to Rod Marsh and the Australian Institute of Sport Cricket Academy in Adelaide. If there's one thing that Rod has drilled into his graduates it's how to go for a big shout in front of the three prongs.

CRICKET LOVERS, hasn't the Australian Cricket Board pulled the right rein with this sizzling hot summer of cricket. Getting the Pakistanis and the Sri Lankans out here to weave their magic against our Ashes-winning crowd was a stroke of pure entrepreneurial genius. The gate crews have been turning the public away in droves from day one. The icing on the cake was the lightning-fast trip from the old traditional rivals, the West Indians.

A note of caution, my very good friends. This may have been the last summer that cricket sold itself on its own merit. As we head into the nineties, we have to look much more closely at how to promote the caper now that soccer has booted off a summer season and now that the heat is on with the bases loaded at the top of the sixth in the baseball brouhaha across the nation, screaming for the leisure dollar. Cricket must learn from the other codes and comps how to promote itself or, like the dinosaur, become too heavy and too stupid to survive.

Look how the rugby league has kicked on since linking up with the great Tina Turner. She pointed out in one brief moment the raw, wild, untamed sex appeal of running round the paddock in shorts week in, week out, in the toughest football competition in the world. Never have blokes, buttocks or balls looked better than when Tina told us that you would be an idiot to yourself if you didn't do everything in your power to bag one of the guys and take him home to your place and get him nude real quick regardless of whether you're male or female.

Of course, cricket couldn't walk this racy road as the innate, conservative nature of the game screams 'WHOA!' before the pants are dropped and the lewd, bang-a-gong, get-it-on sensuality of the players is revealed.

The bottom line is that the nation has had a gutful of souvenir medals, baggy green caps, Greg Chappell slip-slop hats, signed bats, record-breaking balls, team photos and souvenir dollies from the 1956 tour of the subcontinent. To be honest, like you, I have a shed full of that rubbish at home. It's a joke. It's a farce.

Now the ACB brains trust that has whipped Merv into a superstar has shown the way forward with a style of individual promotion that will blast cricket out of the doldrums of the current age and into the twenty-first century.

The breathtaking breakthrough made by the Hughes handlers is that the biggest bloke isn't in the squad for his cricketing skill but for his ability to play the character parts. Merv plays the naive and innocent boofhead from up-country who can't wait to ram his tongue into any hole as soon as the furniture is disturbed. I, for one, can't wait until he graduates from the National Institute of Dramatic Art and can stroll out through the gate and take the new ball from the Punt Road end like Hamlet with a skull tucked down the front of the trousers, or go out hoping to score a lightning-fast fifty as Little John out of Robin Hood with a stump for his staff, or field at mid-on playing the heavy, the Method acting way, with all the clout of Chuck Norris or Sylvester Stallone. In this part he doesn't plant the lips on the mates, but plants the knuckle sandwich on the opposition.

The Merv Hughes think tank hit pay dirt with the shoe ads, the aerobics books, the Merv Hughes bedtime kits, the smoke social appearances and the kiddies' get-work endorsements.

With all this fluff paying the rent, how about a series of audio cassettes to play in the car on the way to the game called 'Musings with Merv'? On these, Merv spills his guts on the big issues that confront the nation, like vegetarianism: how it can work for you; home slaughtering: the pros and cons; Princess Di and panty hose: do they have a future, etc.

The sky's the limit with Merv, because the nexus between results on the paddock and cashflow off it has been broken forever. It will end, where all the great promotions end, with a TV show on top-rating Channel 10 simply called *Merv*.

But having said that, let's open the whole Pandora's box of possibilities. I would kill for an album of songs by Stumpy Boon called 'The Songs of a Short-Leg'. Stumps wouldn't have to open the larynx himself, but he and his advisers could select them. Chestnuts like 'Jump in My Car', 'The Real Thing', 'Funky Town' (the Pseudo Echo arrangement) and 'New York Mining Disaster' would all be sung by the original bands under the baton of the maestro of the willow, one S. Boon. Plus on green vinyl with a red label a bonus single of Stumps having a go at personal favourites like 'Running Bear' and on the flip, 'Has Anyone Seen Old Sid Around?' These would be certified tunes that Boonie sings to himself while fielding in close. There would be a simple film clip with Boonie mouthing a few lyrics while he tonked six after six at the Gabba.

Now I might be wide of the slips cordon but I would love to know how Swampy Marsh passed time camped in the gully day after day.

Marshie's recent dig in a beer commercial has 'rager' written all over it and he must have a volume of verse tucked away in the top drawer just itching to see the light of day. You know the sort of gear—a personal selection of thoughts that kept him going through a summer in Britain. The great thing is that if Marshie hasn't done it, it wouldn't take long to rope in from the boundary any one of a half-dozen cricket writers to do it for him. Names like Blowers, Johnners, Benners, and Lawrers all can write, or at least that's what the blatherings have been telling us for years, and ghosting is perfectly respectable for a busy bloke with a ton on his mind.

THE BOTTOM LINE, MY GOOD FRIENDS, IS THAT THERE IS A GOLDMINE OUT THERE JUST WAITING FOR SOMEONE TO GET OUT AND SHIFT THE OVERBURDEN AND GET ON WITH IT.

THERE IS TOTAL FAILURE WHEN IT COMES TO CAPTURING THE WILD, WACKY WORLD OF THAT ROYAL ZIG AND ZAG DUO, CHARLES AND PRINCESS DI. NO MATTER WHERE YOU PLACE A FIX ON THIS MAD COUPLE THEY'RE OUT THERE PUSHING THE OUTSIDE OF THE FRUIT BAG AND PULLING STUNTS MUCH MORE ROWDY THAN YOU CAN IMAGINE.
I HAVE KNOWN THEM FOR YEARS AND LIKE A COUPLE OF GOOD RED WINES THEY JUST GET BETTER AND BETTER.

TWO LOVE BUBS

IT HAS TURNED OUT UGLY

And now, surprise, surprise, we learn it has been ugly from the off.

My mail is that the whole shebang was doomed from the time the happy couple opened a box of Dark Brown Classics together on their first date and, with the blindfolds on, took turns at playing Pick the Brown using only their sense of taste. It was doomed from the moment the Royal trousers in the form of the Duke, Phil, stuck the Royal bonce round the kitchen door at Balmoral and bellowed, 'Di's the one, sonny jim, and get a wriggle on!'

IT WAS DOOMED from the time the Royal lovebirds sat in the balcony of the Odeon in Leicester Square and the Prince flopped his arm round her shoulders going for upstairs outside while they watched Our Livvy and John Travolta weave their on-screen magic in *Grease*. (Her choice not his.)

IT WAS DOOMED from the time she began to exercise to Human League's 'Love Action' while he consoled himself fiddling about with Elgar's awkward cello riffs on the walkman.

IT WAS DOOMED from the first time their lips touched and he heard the rustle of silk as her thighs rubbed sensuously together.

IT WAS DOOMED long before he said, 'I do,' and she fluffed her lines to the blousily frocked cleric's probing question, buggering up his name

It was doomed from the time the Royal lovebirds sat in the balcony of the Odeon in Leicester Square and the Prince flopped his arm round

ON THE BURST

her shoulders going for upstairs outside while they watched Our Livvy and John Travolta weave their on-screen magic in GREASE. (Her choice not his.)

in reply on the big day all those years ago.

IT WAS DOOMED from the time the honeymoon barge the Royal Yacht *Britannia* pulled out from Portsmouth with the lovely couple plonked between the satin sheets in 'The Charge of the Light Brigade' suite. The only memory either of them have of those fourteen fun-filled days in the Mediterranean is the smell of vomit and of sailors swabbing the decks with Spruce fragrance Pine-O-Cleen. Is it any wonder the whole house of cards has gone for a burton?

IF THOSE SIGNALS OF DANGER WEREN'T TELLING ENOUGH, WE NOW LEARN IT'S BEEN DOOMED SINCE BIRTH. And looking back through the past, with the advantage of twenty-twenty hindsight, it's been doomed for generations. Well, at least as far back as the time Lenin's lads dragged the Czar out of the farmhouse and bumped him off.

LET ME SAY FROM THE JUMP I LOVE THEM ALL. I always have. They're a fun crowd. People who are prepared to swivel the hips whenever Tom Jones's 'It's Not Unusual' is turned up loud on the Palace hi-fi. They love nothing more than downing the tool and rhumbaing around Balmoral whenever someone yells, 'Anyone want a Carr's Tablewater and a top-up of Yalumba Five Crown Port?'

But I come on the job today with the bucket of human kindness and the mop of marital reconciliation wanting to wipe the whiteboard clean and create understanding where previously there was only pain and torment. And I can only do that by setting out the facts and letting those facts tell the story without comment.

HAVING SAID THAT, I DO BLAME MYSELF FOR MUCH OF WHAT HAS HAPPENED OVER THE LAST FORTY YEARS.

THE LOON'S EARLY SPORTING YEARS

You didn't have to be Australia's finest punting mind to see that young Charles was burdened from the off by being born an unwanted kiddie. He was hated at school. I suggested by way of fun that he be introduced to the Royal sports during the school holidays. These sports have kept Royal families together on three continents for generations. But the Duke of Edinburgh got excited and went too far, as usual. PHIL IN LESSON ONE FORCED YOUNG CHARLES, AGED THREE, TO GUT A STILL-FLAPPING BROWN TROUT PLUCKED FROM AN ICY HIGHLAND STREAM. PHIL THEN OFFERED THE BOY THE ENTRAILS FOR BREAKFAST. We all cacked ourselves senseless as the young heir tried to swallow the slimy mess. Later I thought it was too harsh on the lad because if you don't go for the fish caper completely that sort of forced experience does tend to make you feel a bit peaky and you begin to wonder if Dad may be a prong short of the complete fork.

In those days the Duke was always getting around in the tartan skirt and expecting the youngster to do the same day or night, summer or winter. PHIL WORE THE SKIRT BECAUSE IT ALLOWED SO MUCH MORE ACCESS TO WHAT HE CALLED 'THE TRUMPET AREA OF THE ANATOMY' and, as he said, you never knew when a good tune would bob up. But to lock the kiddie into the same mindset from so early on was, I thought, a bit cruel, callous and counterproductive.

Hours of the Prince's life were wasted on the trot beating for pigs across miles of heather in the Scottish Highlands, wearing nothing but one of Dad's old sporrans. Phil, meanwhile, was camped in the warmth of the Royal Range Rover waiting for the porkers to break cover. This is no way for a youngster to spend his end-of-winter term break. You don't go back to school refreshed and eager for a bullying from your schoolmates.

Finally, CHARLES WAS TAUGHT TO SHOOT BY BLAZING AWAY AT NOBBLED HIGHLAND CATTLE WITH THEIR LEGS SAWN OFF AT THE KNEE. This sort of treatment from the jump tends to blow your sense of fun and gets you asking, 'Is there a God?' at a pretty early age.

AUSTRALIA, THE HAPPIEST YEARS OF THE LOON'S LIFE

I could see the kid was getting nowhere at Gordonstoun. I pulled a few strings and got him at the head of the queue into Timbertop. There he thrived. Roy and I could keep an eye on him and he began doing things ● ● ● ●

the Australian way, like CHASING 'ROOS THROUGH THE BUSH NUDE, learning the art of the Flaming Edgar and loving the bonding weekends away in the scrub living with the AID OF ONLY A SWISS ARMY KNIFE AND A BOX OF MATCHES. Magic days.

At night, the lad was locked in after lights out. But he soon learned to participate in traditional amusements. Everyone rolled up copies of the Age newspaper, inserted them date-high, torched them, and took bets on how many circuits of the dorm could be completed BEFORE BURN-OUT AT THE BROWN RING.

The Prince found himself in the freedom the Top allowed. He said to me many years later, 'Thanks for Timbertop, H.G. It's been the only place on the planet I have felt really alive.'

THE POLO YEARS WITH THE HOORAYS HANGING ABOUT

Charles came of age on the loose in swinging London. He has never been completely able to get away and shake the minders' grip. Never able to hoon around the capital and spend a night tooling about looking for love at his own speed.

I tried to get him fixed up with people who would do the right thing. But he wouldn't listen and fell in with that fast-moving polo crowd with their cash, cars, chicken, champagne and double-barrelled surnames.

My influence over him waned and the boy embarrassed himself, his family and his code by continually falling off conveyances mid-chukka. Finally, when he couldn't take it any more, he CHUCKED A WOBBLY

AND BELTED THE HORSE with the business end of the polo mallet.

Throughout all of this the oldies kept putting the hard word on him about getting spliced. Anyone would do as long as she fit the bill—their bill. The Loon could not turn up at the Palace for a romantic evening of Twister with a continental film star, a TV weather presenter or a well-credentialled lassie from the wonderful world of show business without the acid being poured on by the oldies upstairs.

Finally Phil put the foot down. BIG EARS HAD NO SAY IN IT. All he could do was bandage the buttocks nightly and care for the bruises created by Dad's sensitive technique of persuasion. Was this a way to treat a grown man?

IT TAKES TWO TO TANGO

When Roy suggested Lady Di to Prince Philip as a solution to the Palace's dilemma we all had a great laugh. We were rubble when the Duke took us seriously.

It is so easy to bag Di without pausing to think for a minute about the person on the receiving end. She was hurled off the end of the pier iNTO THE SEA OF ROYAL STUPIDITY WITHOUT A LIFE PRESERVER.

Di has done a whole heap of nothing since leaving kindergarten. She sat at home surrounded by stuffed toys she saved from childhood, doing bugger-all, with nowhere to go, no-one to see, and nothing in the appointment book for years.

How long could you take it before you started screaming for help? When you found no-one was listening wouldn't you want to get out and about and add meaning to your life by LASHING OUT IN HARRODS, MARKS AND SPARKS AND TESCOS?

THE THERAPY OF THE WALLET: spend your way to wealth

Wouldn't you think of suicide if you had had the run-outs with the blokes Di has had? Your confidence would be shot. But attempting suicide by sticking your head in the boot of the car and hoping someone drives off without noticing is a very chancy enterprise. Hurling yourself downstairs on the off chance you'll land on a sharp weapon held up by the suit of armour is hoping for the best. Trying to KILL YOURSELF BY EATING CHOCOLATES—well, medical information recently to hand suggests you pass out before doing yourself too much damage.

BUT IT GIVES YOU A CLUE AS TO HOW DESPERATE SHE WAS.

When she presented in the surgery that fateful morning carrying that big handbag of emotional baggage I had to suggest something pretty radical.

I suggested she spend her way out of trouble and find happiness by paying for it. I don't know what made me do it. It was a hunch, I guess. It was part of the thinking of the times. Once Di got familiar with the concept that you could get things simply by handing over lolly she took to it like Roy to rugby league.

She likes to spend cash, I admit it. Who doesn't? No-one in the last fifty years has been able to do the right thing by the British economy the way Princess Di has. She may have SPENT $330,000 ON CLOTHES AND GROOMING LAST YEAR. So what. It included $10,000 on stockings at $50 a pair. That's 200 pairs. A pair every 1.8 days, or a new fit every forty-three hours. Who am I to bag someone who has the very simple need to feel not washed, but new nylons being pulled across their thighs every forty hours or so. Just because I don't feel the need is it any reason to sell someone the dump? Is it any wonder that Di spent $50,000 on facials? In her world you have to pay to be touched by someone who cares. It doesn't come cheap. Di's total fitness hasn't come cheaply either but she is a very fit Royal. THE FITTEST ROYAL SINCE GEORGE THE THIRD IN FACT and that's a big rap, a very big rap.

A PRINCESS IN LOVE (simply the facts)

Author Anna Pasternak was doing nothing so I whispered the word 'novel' into her ear some years ago over a couple of wines and a plate of crumbed offal and obviously this whisper got her thinking about making up stories. It must have been in the blood—after all, she was connected to Boris. The result—A PRINCESS IN LOVE. WHAT A READ! What a fiction! But for mine it doesn't ring true. There are no details of Di's world that make me think, Hullo, gentleman Jimmy Hewitt really was there and Anna has been told (continuing revelations notwithstanding).

For instance, there is no mention of Kim Beazley anywhere in the 743 pages. I don't think I'm breaking any news when I reveal that Di's lovers include Kim Beazley. Fact!

Di has referred to Kim in secret phone-tapped tapes that have come into my possession as KIMMIE, BIG BOY, FLUTEMAN, TIGER, TOOLEY, TUGGER, TICKY, TWO TOOLS, BEAZERS, BEAZ-O, BLURTER, BODGIE, THE BOOTLE and HOT HOOLEY. And don't those nicknames have the ring of authenticity and intimacy. I honestly don't know how Kim found the time. But their omission from the book reveals A Princess in Love a joke. Nothing more than a thigh-high fishnet stocking of implausibility unravelling just below the suspender belt.

THE BOUNDER FROM THE HOUSEHOLD CAVALRY, 'ON THE JOB' JAMES

I can't steer you right with regards to the third sharp point of this triangle, James Hewitt. Obviously, I, like many others, have admired his work in the NIGHT TOOL DEPARTMENT for many years. He remains a mystery man, a mystery to me, a mystery to Princess Di and, surprisingly, a mystery to himself.

I was lucky enough to get a few words for Australian readers from James Hewitt's French hideaway pigsty this week. I got there ahead of the tabloid curve for an exclusive. JUNGLE JIM HAS BEEN HOLED UP IN A PIG PEN WITH HIS MUM DISGUISED AS A PIG FARMER VETTING ALL CALLERS. She gave me the wink and eased the way in. I FOUND

THE CAD LURKING ON ALL FOURS SNOUT DEEP IN THE TROUGH. He bellowed at me from both ends, 'What are you looking at, H.G.? Tell all your fellow Asians I have never had it so good and bugger me, H.G., I doubt I will ever get it this good again!'

James then introduced me to a couple of his recently acquired chums in the next sty. I immediately recognised the quartet as Australian prime export porker. I had last seen this lot Warialda way with Noel and Les Cleal and a couple of big dogs in hot pursuit. James was in good company and seemed to be making the best of his continental run of outs. I left none the wiser but was pleased to renew some old acquaintances.

PHIL THE GREEK BREAKS COVER AND COMES OUT SWINGING

At least these events have flushed out Prince Philip into the open. What a tremendous role model the old bloke turns out to be, generous to a fault and so understanding.

I tracked 'Old Rodger' down to one of the games rooms round the back of Balmoral just before the off to Russia. HE SPOKE TO ME AT LENGTH THROUGH THE TRADESMEN'S ENTRANCE between blasts of the double-barrelled shotgun at some cornered pheasants. 'H.G., tell them across Asia that despite the way we've done it, everything has been done for the benefit of the country. It's not for our benefit.'

Strange comment from the Duke, and as he turned to draw a bead on a hapless water buffalo that had been wheeled in by the game keeper I was left thinking that no wonder the joint is buggered if this is an example of the rapidly weakening grip on the reality lever at the top.

A BED IN THE HOLIDAY HOUSE – THEIRS FOR THE ASKING

These are the facts as I know them. I allow you to make your own judgment. I am much wiser for my involvement with this crowd of losers, but I still consider them all to be my friends and if they ever bob up wanting a bed down at the weekender, I'LL DO MY BEST TO SQUEEZE THEM IN.

A Night On the Bong with Viv Squeezed Into the Tartan Wedding Dress

Mambo will put <u>2</u> eggs in every garage by the year 2 thousand

I CAME TO THE FASHION CAPER AS A VERY LATE BLOOMER. Once I got a sniff of what the card had to offer, I rusted on. There is something so completely twentieth century about the whole idea of pants made by very big names featuring very big labels with very big price tags being promoted on the hips of very slim people to be stretched over the very big buttocks of the buyers. Vivacious Vivienne Westwood has a lot of knockers but I won't hear a word against her. She was there at the birth of punk finding a way to make a quid out of bin liners, bondage trousers and sticking safety pins through the nose and that is good enough for me.

When I got the call late last night from the secret hideaway love nook of the 100% Mambo Surf-realists asking me to spill my blood with regards to getting the balloon above the guttering for this catalogue, I was blown away. I turned to rubble. I was cactus. But being an art buff, even though it was 4.30 am I downed the night tool. Got out of bed. Rushed to a blank sheet of A4 paper and began ploughing up the page with a Pentel pen.

Where can you start with this crew of gutsy Australians who have, for mine, created an art movement as lively and as shattering of the artistic mould as cubism? That is a big rap, a bloody big rap. But who else in the history of art can you compare the Surf-realists with? They are all goers. There is plenty of drive from the back of the palette. They bring to art the four great ingredients of the caper: commitment, imagination, energy and, above all, arousal. And remember, the long suit at 100% Mambo is arousal. Don't be surprised if you find yourself calling for a chair as you take a peek at these doozies.

AS YOU MAKE YOUR WAY ROUND THE EXHIBITION THINK OF THE DAY LEONARDO DA VINCI HURLED *THE LAST SUPPER* UP ONTO THE REFECTORY WALL, SNIPPED THE RIBBON, PULLED THE BLACK SHROUD AWAY AND ASKED THE LOCAL TEAM OF TASTEMAKERS AND CRITICS IN FOR A SHUFTI.

Don't tell me that as you confront these Mambo works and have your suspicions of genius confirmed that you aren't experiencing exactly the same emotions as that gang of Neville Nobodies who turned up at Leonardo's unveiling all those years ago. There is joy, amazement, surprise bordering on the religious plus a very delicate but palpable hint of revulsion which is contained in all great art—and don't be surprised if there is a distinct movement in the trouser area.

Art buffs, the lasting thing about the Mambo movement is that they have collectively taken the Free the Art Gallery Movement of yesteryear to its logical conclusion. Not only have they pulled art off the gallery walls, where no-one was taking a geek, but they have plonked it on our backs for all to see.

Now I was sharing a bong the other night with the very talented fashion designer Vivienne Westwood. This was after a vigorous high C had been chimed on the bed flutes. As we tidied up, the talk turned to art and the big twentieth-century movements. Viv rates this current Mambo gear 'rave up' (her term not mine) as one step shy of her best work, which she maintains was a torn Glad binliner done up with a packet of safety pins plonked on a dead punk's head which was hung in the Tate in December 1978. That is very high praise indeed for someone in the know, who is still bagging the big prizes and pulling all the head and the majority of knowledgeable plaudits.

Viv stressed to me, as she re-stoked the cone, that all great fashion art belongs on the floor. Her telling words were, **'H.G., ALL THAT LUSCIOUSLY SUMPTUOUS GEAR KNOCKED UP BY CRAZY KARL LAGERFELD AND THE BIG O, OSCAR DE LA RENTA, AND FLASHED ON THE PLANKS BY NAOMI, CINDY AND THE REST OF THE SUPERMODELS**

COUNTS FOR ZILCH WHEN IT COMES OFF AND IS HURLED INTO THE NEAREST CROCK AS BEING NEXT TO USELESS IN THE LOVE ARTS AT THE BUSINESS END OF THE EVENING.'

Her analysis and insight took my breath away.

Viv and I whiled away the rest of the evening discussing whether da Vinci was an overrated sick joke or simply an art dud.

As the dawn broke with a blistering pink and puce sunrise, a rooster began to scream in an upper-register Esperanto that I barely understood. My dayglo lime green EJ Holden with a blowfly-blown engine pulled into the yard of its own accord and as I got in behind the wheel my boardshorts were flapping at halfmast from the sloop. Viv bellowed to me as I pulled out of the drive, 'H.G., the Mambo Surf-realists connect the head, the heart, the buttocks and the night tools. Then they pour it all into a pair of pants. Now piss off, short stuff, I've got a spring collection to create.'

I left for a very sobering drive back to the smoke. I cleared the Hills Hoist in Viv's backyard just in time to see the B52s pounding the nearby hills.

As I left the sticks behind I mumbled a brief prayer to triangular eye in the noon-day sky and it dawned on me that THE SOUND THAT MAKES THE ARTIST GIGGLE IS THE SOUND OF THE HAT BEING HURLED IN THE AIR, THE SHIRT BEING RIPPED FROM THE BACK, THE CLANG OF DUDS BANGING ON THE FLOOR, THE SOUND OF THE WHOLE BRASS BAND TURNING UP FOR AN ENCORE PERFORMANCE.

In fact, the very sounds of 100% Mambo Art.

My very good friends, you have in your hands a thorough and complete map to this magnificent exhibition. Congratulations on discovering total optical enjoyment. But remember, if you don't give a bugger about art why not let your duds do the talking for you? They are probably a lot more eloquent than you could ever be and who knows, you might spot another pair talking your language here in this very gallery.

BEATING THE CUT IN THE LONG KIKUYU OF THE LITHGOW LINKS

ROY'S 'GRIP IT AND
RIP IT' style came
into its own as
the pillows
powdered and the big
man bagged the half full,
cut glass sherry decanter up
for grabs at the Lithgow Open.
He stopped the world on the
seventeenth when he pulled the pin
out of the hole, teed off on the last
using the flag as a driver and plonked
the hot dot on the green pin high.
Even the Shark stopped talking, briefly.

94

THE STORY STARTS IN THE PANTS

I'm not the first person in the history of the caper to say this, but Australian golf is teetering on the brink of chaos. Classics around the nation have been given the bullet. Prize money is being mauled as the big sponsors duck and run for cover. The recession has put the cleaners through the on-course pro-shop tills. Even the Sunday hackers are being squeezed off links around the nation by avalanches of golf-mad tourists of all persuasions tumbling legless off Boeing 747s primed for a big hit at your local.

Our great players, recent British Open successes notwithstanding, are on the back foot. The Dark Shark, I. B-Finch, is reduced to pulling the pants off in every difficult lie in a desperate bid to get someone, anyone, to notice he's out there somewhere, having a swing. Rodger Davis is pinning all his hopes on a pair of unwashed, antique plus-fours which he wears for superstitious reasons, having bagged some minor-grade gorgonzola cheese in those attractive daks years earlier.

And the Shark? Well, before his British Open win, Greg went into the room of mirrors, stopped talking to anyone with a pencil and pad, left it alone for at least a day, and had a good hard look at himself. He asked the hard questions, like: 'Who am I?'; 'What is golf?'; 'What is a Shark?'; 'Where is my date?'; 'What do I do?' His BO success was solely due to the fact that when he asked himself 'Who am I?', the Great White answered, in a moment of blistering lucidity, 'Jack Nicklaus'.

The only other insight into the Shark's magnificent showing

95

Don't tell me you wouldn't travel miles to see a new-look links that had crocs and piranhas lurking in the water hazards, tarantulas in every bunker and big-game traps placed strategically around every tree, with the whole shebang mined by the skills of a terrorist bomber, and TNT and Semtex just waiting to go pop.

at Royal St George's is that if you give an orang-outang a word processor and an endless supply of bananas, it will eventually knock out a masterpiece like Noddy And Big Ears Get A Dog. Golf is just the same. Give a chimpanzee a bag of Cobra clubs, a pair of Niblicks, a hot dot and enough time, and eventually it will throw off the perfect round of golf. The fact that a human being did it, well, I stand here pantless as a mark of respect.

But the news is not all bad. We can arrest this appalling slice into the rough that Australian golf is experiencing by simply introducing a missing ingredient into the game. That ingredient is *violence*.

The forgotten fact of golf is that it can be an incredibly violent game. Don't tell me that the ordinary punter, the big skins players and the sponsorship elephant dollars would not be wooed back to the great game if we could offer the golf-crazed public the sight of a world's number one, crazed with a case of the yips, wrapping the shaft of his broomstick putter three times around the hapless caddie's neck when a metre putt is missed in a desperate bid to make par and win a major tournament. Don't tell me you wouldn't travel miles to see a new-look links that had crocs and piranhas lurking in the water hazards, tarantulas in every bunker and big-game traps placed strategically around every tree, with the whole shebang mined by the skills of a terrorist bomber, and TNT and Semtex just waiting to go pop.

Don't tell me that you wouldn't scream, 'Yes, I want to be there and see that! I want to see someone go crazy, mad or broke! I want to be there for the Big Bang!'

96

It was that great Australian pro of the seventies, Rampaging Roy Slaven, who persuaded me that violence was golf's missing ingredient. I first saw Roy giving a golf course a red-hot poke when he was swinging the bag at the 1978 Golden Offal Tray, as the Lithgow Open was called. The trophy was a beautiful selection of still-warm, freshly killed sweetmeats covered with a substantial layer of gold. 'The Big O' or 'the Offal', as the Lithgow Open has always been called, is a popular trophy with the world's top professionals, and the 1978 BO was the best ever.

THE OFFAL'S ON THE TURN AND THE FLIES ARE BUZZING

The first two days of the Offal were played in atrocious conditions as remnants of Cyclone Curry-Kenny lashed the course. The driving rain and impenetrable fog reduced visibility to a mere 3.6 metres. Radar was on loan from the nearby Richmond RAAF base to find some of the more difficult lies in the rough.

Roy started badly. His long game was pathetic. His short game was a joke. He missed the cut, but immediately appealed to the championship committee for a wild card entry into the final rounds.

Unfortunately, at the end of day two, Jack Nicklaus was run over in the car park after carding a course record 12-under-par. With Jack laid up in the local hospital, and given that Roy represented the major sponsors—ie, the Slaven Nelson Group of Companies—the championship committee didn't take long to see the wisdom of giving Roy another go. (Incidentally, when the matter of the Nicklaus accident came to court, Roy said he just didn't see Jack bending over as he reversed out in his V8 Kingswood ute.)

A SECOND SNIFF OF THE OFFAL WAS ALL ROY NEEDED

The next morning dawned with perfect weather for golf. But Roy couldn't escape drama. He spent the night in Sydney at a rugby league awards night, where he scooped the best and fairest pool and was inducted into the Hall of Fame for his contribution to the art of ● ● ● ●

head-high tackling and going the grope.

Roy's luck, however, was about to run out. His trusty Kingswood broke down on the way back to Lithgow the following morning. The gear-box went at exactly the same time as the head gasket and the fuel line snapped at a set of lights in Norton Street, Leichhardt. The car was buggered. Roy took all day to walk from Sydney to the course carrying his bag. He teed off at about 5.30 pm, just as the leaders were arriving at the nineteenth.

ROY RIPS IT AND GRIPS IT

In the twilight, Roy began his quest for the Offal with an act of violence that set the tone for a brilliant two days of competition. He pulled a wriggling length of reptile out of the bottom of his bag, bit the head off and munched. Roy maintained there was nothing like the head of a taipan for getting the liver off his spleen. It was also just the tonic for good golf.

Roy needed a pick-me-up. In the '78 Offal, his game was handicapped by a dickie ticker, a cracked sternum, a groin ripped clean from the bone and flute injuries which would have made any other competitor weep. These injuries were suffered during the recently completed football season and prevented him from swinging a club above waist height. The deadly snake came from the Wallerawang Reptile Park where it was surplus to requirements. It was, however, returned to them the very next day in mint condition, minus the head.

The gearbox went at exactly the same time as the head gasket and the fuel line snapped at a set of lights in Norton Street, Leichhardt. The car was buggered. Roy took all day to walk from Sydney to the course carrying his bag.

98

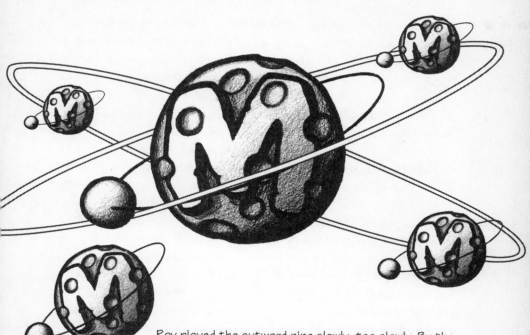

Roy played the outward nine slowly—too slowly. By the time he turned, one under the card, night had descended. Roy didn't stop for a moment. He began tearing the course apart. He played from memory with the aid of the luminous dials on his watch and the sputtering light of a hurricane lamp that he always slung between the wheels of the buggy for this sort of emergency.

Roy approached the tenth with trepidation. It was a vicious 388-metre dog-leg par five that lay out there, somewhere in the dark, intent on ruining his chances in the Offal. To help him, he called for a napalm airstrike to illuminate the course. When the RAAF F111s arrived and laid the flaming jelly down, Roy teed off and bagged an eagle.

The Slaven Slaughterhouse, as Roy's supporters were called, went wild. They hooted and hollered when the wall of flame went up, taking with it a few nearby houses. They loved the smell of napalm. It smelt like victory in the evening.

Roy electrified the vast crowd when he strangled a platypus with his bare hands on the thirteenth to calm his nerves before attempting a monster pin-high putt from fifty-seven metres to save par. A lot of people found it hard to accept, the wanton destruction of such a lovely creature simply for the purpose of carding a good score. But, in Roy's defence, he's a genius playing the game at the highest level. Who can argue with his motivational techniques, as long as the results are on the scoreboard? It might be said, though, that Roy went a bit far on the fifteenth when he used a wombat as a flute warmer.

Undoubtedly the highlight of Roy's magic round was on the eighteenth when he had to drop the hot dot in from eighteen-and-a-half metres without the aid of the hurricane lamp which, by this stage, had run out of fuel. Roy simply selected a club, addressed the ball, examined the lie, and calmly dropped his togs—I. B-Finch-style—before letting one go from the back door, lighting it up with a match, and sinking the putt using his own fuel to illuminate the green.

The Slaughterhouse went gaga. Chaired by deliriously happy fans, Roy emerged from the night with a card of three-under and the promise of a strong challenge for the Offal winner's puce and date-brown jacket.

THE OFFAL GOES OFF

For the final round on the following day, an Australasian record crowd was on hand to see the Golden Offal climax. When Roy arrived there were two things on his mind—winning and violence. It couldn't be the raw brutality and savagery of the previous night. All the contestants were well aware that Roy had scorched the course in the gloom. Roy knew it would be a day which called for the worst sort of violence—mind violence. This was just as he liked it. Roy just loved the game when it was played upstairs.

The leaders going into round four, well, Roy hated them all. There was 'Laughing' Lee Trevino, Nick Faldo (down in the dumps and on the mope as usual), and the super-Spaniard Seve Ballesteros with twin brother Cisco to carry the bag. Roy was four strokes behind Lee and just one behind Nick and Seve, who were locked together in second spot. Roy pulled the initiative right from the start, arriving at the first tee in bright red high heels, a date-brown suspender belt, fish-nets, and a Tina Turner-style fright wig plonked down hard above the lippy and rouge. He was dressed for the round of his life. And when Roy makes the effort, he's a real head-turner. Slaven went in hard early. As Seve placed the ball on the first tee, Roy trod on it with his high

arriving at the first tee in bright red high heels, a date-brown suspender belt, fish-nets, and a Tina Turner-style fright wig plonked down hard above the lippy and rouge

heels. It sank 16 cm into the soft turf, giving Seve a particularly difficult lie before a stroke was even made. Roy spotted Trevino's bag and simply laid a serve of brown carpet all over Laughing Lee's clubs. Lee saw the funny part, which was good, but by the time he played the third hole, he couldn't see the course because he was covered in flies. Roy applied the Christmas handshake to Faldo when they shook hands which let Nick know in the most convincing fashion Roy was there.

Roy stepped up to the tee and 'buttocked' his first drive. If you haven't seen Roy buttock a drive, stop him in the street next time you see him and ask him to demonstrate. He simply places the ball, selects a club, turns his back, drops his togs, inserts the wood into an alluring bit of crack, wriggles the hips and takes a dip while amusing the Slaughterhouse with card tricks. On this occasion the ball ended smack-bang in the middle of the fairway, 320 metres away, and it was on for the next eighteen holes. Roy cleared his throat, gave a heave and laid a bushman's handkerchief into Faldo's bag as the four approached the second. Nick was having trouble with club selection. The genius of Roy's tactic meant that whenever Nick dipped into the bag and pulled a length clear, the club emerged dripping with a Mervyn Hughes-style phlegm that dripped all over Nick's shoes and stuck the ball to the club. Faldo was history.

Roy began moving up the scoreboard. Picking up two strokes on the outward nine and sensing victory on the way back to the clubhouse, Roy began leaving small pieces of brown carpet strategically on the green where opponents couldn't help but step in them. Seve copped the red-back spider treatment on the eighth and was reduced to a yabbering wreck, unable to complete the round. Roy pulled to the lead by eating a packet of crisps as Lee was about to swing on the tenth.

Throughout the round, Roy's sledging was brilliant. When Roy works blue, everyone stops and listens. He tooled up on the green and blew the opposition away by strapping the putter to the flute and sinking eight-metre putts with his hands in the air. He would save par by putting his hands down the front of his trousers and poking them through the open fly to get a firm grip on the shaft and to calm his nerves.

On the eighteenth, Roy was three up and the Offal was his. He arrived on the last green early having hit a monster drive off the tee, and calmly pulled a loaded shotgun from the back of the bag where most players keep an umbrella. Roy has always maintained that if you want to win at golf, it's wise to carry something which exudes authority. There's nothing players find more aggravating than someone like Roy standing around with a double-barrelled sawn-off taking a bead at their wedding tackle as they walk up to the final green.

In his victory speech, Roy was at his gracious and charitable best. 'Ladies and gentlemen, I've always loved the Offal. I have always wanted to win. I love this winner's jacket. All I will say to my fellow competitors is thanks for coming and thanks for being a bunch of jokes and powdering when the going got tough.'

Suddenly the big man was gone, but his deeds in the Offal have made certain that violence and golf will be linked forever.

In a single championship, Roy showed us the future.

Just Another Chook To Be Hypnotised

- THE POLITICAL PROCESS COMES ALIVE WHEN THE BIG BLOKES PULL ON SUITS, GO TO THEIR CORNERS AND PRETEND THEY'RE TELLING US SOMETHING MEANINGFUL. ON THE BIG NIGHT, THE TV CHANNEL THAT SHOWS A REPEAT OF THE DIRTY DOZEN WINS THE RUGGED RATINGS BATTLE HANDS DOWN, SUCH IS THE INTEREST IN THIS HYPNOTIC ELECTORAL DOUBLE ACT.

The New Year has bolted out of the shed with the donk ablaze up front, the pedal is pressed hard to metal and it promises to be a wild ride even with the seat belts done up tight.

The icing on the cake of 1993 is the forthcoming federal election. The electorate is in a difficult position, being offered a stark

103

trout eyes

choice, a very stark choice, between proven failure and potential disaster. What has got me revved up are these promised debates between the big two.

I want to see a genuine debate, a genuine stoush between the PM Paul Keating and his opposite number 'the Nightripper' Doctor John Hewson. But I don't want another brouhaha about interest rates, motor vehicle registrations, unemployment, the housing start figures, etc, etc. I pray to see the lads go round facing genuine hands-on tasks that would give us some idea of why we're voting for either of them.

I am therefore proposing a new format for these debates that will not only revolutionise the electorate's impressions of our leaders, but will change forever the political process itself.

Debate number one would be the clown debate. This gives the electorate a chance to assess just how good Paul and John are at entertaining kiddies. My private polling on behalf of Slaven Polls of some twenty thousand Australians on the phone last night found that the entertaining kiddies question is the number one priority with 94.7% of the electorate.

Picture this . . . **the gun goes off, the terrible two come out on the crazy bikes dolled up in clown suits with the very, very funny cardboard top hats. They warm up the madly excited crowd with a bit of magic–the coin in the matchbox, the Chinese rings, the rope with seven ends**, all oldies but goodies—and when the audience is screaming for more, they take listeners' requests organised by a panel of heavy-hitters in the political caper, such as Peter Harvey, Alan Ramsey and Laurie Oakes. After the break they pull on the funny shoes, walk the slack rope, saw each other in half, do the pantomime horse, pluck the juggling balls out of their back doors and as the crowd goes berserk they disappear in the cloud of smoke created by torching their hair.

A listeners' phone poll on the 0055 number would score the night and give the waiting breathless world an immediate result.

The second debate is a double header. The first part is staged underwater and will at last answer the questions we all have wanted asked during the past year. Can Paul catch a mullet? Can Hewie lure a sooty grunter to the side of the boat? Can either leader tickle a trout to death? Can the Big H or the Super K snare a salmon without a skerrick of bait? What can they do with a flathead in the kitchen? Do they let the fish see the greens when serving?

How would they deal with a couple of Vic Hislop super specials? (Vic has promised to provide for this debate a couple of big fish who are red-hot goers and proven killers.)

This debate will be filmed underwater on the Great Barrier Reef.

There'll be six doors plonked on the bottom with big coloured numbers tacked on. Behind each door is a fish and a problem. Paul and John take turns in asking debate master Martin Di Stasio for a door and Adriana Xenides, looking a million dollars in the pink and lime-green wettie, swims over and opens it up. Then Paul or John with only their wits and fishing ability deal with the problems created by their choice.

The second half of debate number two focuses on the meat trade. It would be simply magnificent television to see the two lads, dressed in the navy blue aprons with stripes, wade in and pull a live sheep out of the holding pens at the Berrima Abattoir, slit its throat, bleed it, string it up, pull the hide, get the guts out, go in hard for the offal and then fill an order for a couple of legs, a plate of brains and two kilos of shoulder chops. Top judges from the meat industry would award points for neatness, time taken, presentation and cleanliness.

Finally, the third debate—no real surprises here—is the nude debate. The approved idea for the final debate sees the two contestants strolling out from behind the big black curtain at the Flinders Tennis Centre, chock-a-block full with madly enthusiastic Liberal and Labor supporters, with nothing on, absolutely nothing on.

Once the laughter has died down from the vast crowd on hand, the big two stand around taking questions from a well-dressed cross-section of the Australian community on technique between the sheets with the bed flutes. They'll start off with stumpers like: how much foreplay do you employ? Do you go in hard early? Do you like coming from behind? Do you respect your partner in the morning? Do you smoke afterwards?

These questions are to be set by a panel comprising Fred Nile, Wally Lewis and Imran Khan, and what this trio doesn't know about the sex caper is not worth knowing.

These debates offer three real chances to go beyond the war of words and provide us with genuine insights into these bright sparks, and to see them in action under the pressure of real competition.

And who is to say that a bloke who is not afraid to stand nude before us, who can amuse kiddies, who can drop a steer, who can cook up a big piece of barramundi, is not, in this day and age, the perfect man to lead us into the middle of the decade?

• • • pre-celtic burial chamber.

THE 26 EASY-TO-FOLLOW STEPS OF RUGBY LEAGUE VIOLENCE

I love big, fit blokes going in hard early and often and calling it sport. But there is a price. That price is stupidity. This is a do-it-yourself, cut-out-and-keep guide to an on-going, festering, underbubbling canker that is rugby league's greatest asset. It needs updating hourly. This snapshot was taken in 1993 on the eve of State of Origin Number 2.

A is for **ARKO**, 'the rugby league dreamer'; and **ANGRY PILLS**, as in Trevor 'the Axe' Gillmeister when he's 'chock-a-block full of angry pills'.

B is for the **BRICK WITH EYES**; the **BUTTOCKS**; and **BACK DOOR BENNY**, three of the **BLUES'** best.

C is for the **CAULDRON** of Lang Park; and for **COOSBANE**, a planet visited by players after they take a punch to the head.

D is for **DIZZY GILLESPIE**, aka Cement, a brick wall for the Blues; and **DRUGS** outlawed by the League but still the game's major sponsor.

E is for the **ELE-PHANT GUN** to be used on the losing team who played like a hapless bunch of water buffaloes stuck in the mud waiting for the safari to arrive and put them out of their misery.

F is for **FLATTENED**, as in the prone position in which trainers, club doctors and St John's Ambulance people discover players after a big hit.

G is for **GROIN**: easy to inflame but needs a cold spoon or cold shower or party pack of ice in club colours to soothe.

H is for **HALF-TIME**, a momentary lull for

oranges when the punching stops.

I is for **INJURY**, which rarely happens in State of Origin football.

J is for **JUMPER**, the Maroon football jumper being a well-known aphrodisiac.

K is for **KING HIT** in back play, unseen by the ref and touch judges but clearly seen by everyone at home.

L is for **LARRY DOOLEY**, as in 'the Axe gave the Brick a bit of Larry Dooley in that big hit'.

M is for **MAD**, a state of mind which helps you when you play.

N is for **NUT**, as in 'lay on a bit of nut with a glorious headbutt'. Sadly, a skill missing from Origin football but sure to make a comeback in the Tests against the Poms.

O is for **ORIGIN** and

ONGOING SAGA, as in the 'ongoing saga of league violence in Origin matches'.

P is for **PROMOTION**, which can never adequately capture the raw, brutal and gratuitous violence of the greatest game of all.

Q is for **QUAYLE**; and **QUAINT**, which describes the ARL's attitude towards violence.

R is for **RUCK**, where incidental and random violence can erupt.

S is for **SQUIRREL GRIP**, aka the Christmas handshake, aka the Nairobi night-time grope.

T is for **TUG AND TOOL**, as in give the tool a tug, a favourite post-hooter activity in the rooms; and for **TRADITIONAL SOFTENING-UP PERIOD**, an integral part of any game of league.

U is for **UNDER-PANTS**, the big pants-sized jobs with the extra gusset that fits it all in.

V is for **VIOLENCE**, an obsession of the media and rarely seen on the paddock; and **VOMIT**, the overflow of cream and little bits of carrot that splashes your footy boots when you punch a player hard enough.

W is for **WHITE LINE FEVER**, an affliction that strikes all great players on State of Origin nights.

X is for **X-RAY**, needed to show that a player is busted and then on the mend.

Y is for **'YOU BEAUTY'**, bellowed when one of them is stretchered off and your side scores.

Z is for **ZONKED**, an accurate description of players after eighty minutes of hostilities.

'And the Winners are . . .

MICHAEL HUTCHENCE and PAULA YATES,' IN THE INTERNATIONAL YEAR OF ROMANCE

I love seeing people go crazy and broke, especially when the pants are around the ankles, the flutes are blowing high Cs and the tune is that old favourite, 'Romance'. 1995 was a bumper year. The world's jaded wedding tackle came alive when love, lunacy and loons were let loose for those magical 365 days of the year.

1995 – LOVE IS IN THE AIR

Horizontal folk dancers and bed flautists, I want to take a few minutes of your valuable time to pack down for a pow wow about love because today, 1995, the International Year of Romance, climaxes across the world with a number of star-studded ceremonies that salute the achievements of lovers this year. These functions will reach a fitting conclusion with the crowning in Rome of the Couple of the Year for 1995.

Like many of you I was sceptical when the United Nations burst out of the shed in January and bellowed, '1995, it's the Year of Romance!' to a tight-lipped ashen-faced world. I had serious doubts about it working. But the UN big cheese, Boutros Boutros-Ghali, has asked me to pass on his thoughts about the International Year of Romance. Boo Boo's words were simply, 'Tell them, H.G., it's been a rip snorter!' That is a big rap from a man who has seen a lot of UN-style international years come and go. ● ● ●

111

Incidentally, in Urdu astrology it's been the Year of the Trouser. And when Romance and the Trouser collide in the same calendar year look out for a very loud bang. From that perspective the last twelve months have not disappointed.

Let's have a shufti at this year's card. BOB and BLANCHE'S wedding is an

It was one of those occasions when Bob let his nose do the talking. The hooter said a whole heap more than mere words could have.

enormous strawberry on top of the attractively-baked cake of Romance that is 1995. Will we ever see the nation more united or more certain that romance has a place in our world than on that marvellous day when Bob and Blanche said, 'I do'? And when the happy couple came out to answer questions from the world's press on that joyous mid-winter's day, you'll recall that Bob didn't have much to

say but expressed his emotions by crying through his nose. It was one of those occasions when Bob let his nose do the talking. The hooter said a whole heap more than mere words could have. Talk about memories that will live with us forever.

But it hasn't only been the seniors setting the pace in the International Year of Romance. Hasn't that fun-loving young Australian duo JULIAN McMAHON and DANNII MINOGUE set a wonderful example of how marriage can really work in this day and age!

Despite very heavy work schedules, career pressures and living in countries five hours' flying-time apart, Dan and Jules have been able to see each other twice in the past twelve months. And look at what they have been able to achieve by this very, very post-modern arrangement.

Dannii Minogue's *Playboy* shoot certainly blew everyone away in this the IYOR. There was heartache for hubby Julian McMahon when Dannii signalled to a breathless world that she

112

would tog off and have a go at being Miss August for *Playboy*. was cactus for weeks. The first person I rang was Julian. His muted response was, 'H.G., if it makes her happy, why not?' And you can't argue with that.

What a revealing set of snaps they were! Revealing . . . well, bugger-all, as near as I could tell. Don't get me wrong, I like to exercise to pictures, but the August issue of *Playboy* was a bumper issue from the readers' viewpoint with many very fine articles that seemed, on balance, to overshadow the art.

Senior staff photographer RAMPAGING ROY SLAVEN shot the best part of forty thousand rolls of Kodak Gold ASA 200 to come up with this spread of a dozen happy snaps. And what magic inspiration from Roy. There was Dannii standing around in big boots, Dannii twirling an umbrella, Dannii with a big hat stuck on her bonce, Dannii sporting a pair of tripe bathers. Oh no, Roy pulled out all stops on this one. So much skill! So much sheer inventive-ness! Roy said it was the hardest shoot he had ever

marching to hell with trumpet & drum

undertaken. His brief was 'a little dollop of lewd without being cruelled by the crude', and, by jiminee, I think he nailed it.

The story of Dannii's shoot will be a major project to be financed by the Film Finance Corporation (FFC) in 1996. The Corporation is prepared to fund the proposal to the tune of $6.7 million. It will be filmed under the title of *It's a Joke!*

It's a Joke! will feature BRAD PITT as Roy, MERYL STREEP as Dannii and in the pivotal role of Julian we are pleased to announce that today we have secured the services of MACAULAY CULKIN. As you can see, there is a very Australian feel to the casting.

A lot of people tell me it's hard to get money out of the FFC, but their generosity with the $6.7 million overwhelmed us, as we only asked for $250,000. All we did was submit a treatment of *It's a Joke!* Roy roughed out the basics on a

● ● ● ●

beer coaster one night in the Bloodhouse Hotel, Lithgow. We included a cover letter that said nothing much more than, 'Dear FFC. Gisa the money you sucks or we'll dong you!' The FFC really respond to that sort of rowdy gear and the genius of our application was that we signed it 'Yours sincerely, DAVID PUTTNAM'.

So the legacy of this magnificent year will live on through It's a Joke!

1995 – IT WAS THE BEST FIELD EVER

But this International Year of Romance has been blessed with so many great couples. MELANIE GRIFFITHS and ANTONIO BANDERAS spring to mind. Two love bubs so right, so electric, so hot. (I understand mineral giant BHP is thinking of using them as fuel for their smelting process as they operate at white-hot temperatures that conventional fuels just don't reach. So typical of BHP, always thinking about the environment!)

Melanie said to me not long after she bumped into Antonio,

In the end we had to send Roy in with an ice-cold spoon, a hose attached to a cold water tap and a large crowbar to prise them apart so that production could continue.

'H.G., one look and I was his. And, H.G., he's so much hotter than Don.' And Melanie would be one of the few people on the planet to know about Don. I was on the set when they first met and the director couldn't get them out of the trailer for their nude scenes. In the end we had to send Roy in with an ice-cold spoon, a hose attached to a cold water tap and a large crow-bar to prise them apart so that production could continue.

1995 has been a year full of romantic surprises. For instance, the former DUCHESS and DUKE OF YORK appear to have found romance again. Randy Andy and Fergs are back on the job after three days at

114

an intense horizontal twist workshop in Spain just up the road from CHRISTOPHER SKASE's hacienda-style love nook. Chris popped in from time to time just to make sure Fergie and Andy remembered what went where. When it comes to the love arts no-one knows more about romance than Chris.

Speaking of surprises, MICHAEL JACKSON and LISA MARIE PRESLEY found it hard adjusting to the demands of marriage, but when they hit a rough patch they came up with a very inventive solution. Mid-way through the year Michael thought Lisa Marie looked down in the dumps and so he packed her off to the Hawaiian Islands where she found bliss in the arms of her ex-husband Danny Keough. And now there is even talk of a young Presley-Jackson-Keough on the way. What a marvellous example Michael and Lisa Marie set the kiddies just starting out on life's rich adventure!

Speaking of odd solutions, what about the turmoil that tumbled LIZ HURLEY and HUGH GRANT's way this year? Their love had been put to the test on the black leather seat of a BMW, and now Liz is battling MARLON BRANDO over a $2-million Irish weekender. And who is to say love won't flourish here, reaching out across the generations? It wouldn't be the first time that real estate has brought a couple together.

And then there's DEMI MOORE and BRUCE WILLIS. They didn't down the tools for a minute in 1995. Demi, with the $12-million body (and I can see where every dollar has been spent), and Bruce, with his $9.50 bald head, have single-handedly redefined romance in the nineties, doing crazy things like moving out, moving back in, Bruce being caught with a stripper in a biker's bar. Moving back out. Demi making a film about strippers. Moving back in. In the Willis-Moore stable it's all go. And it's all Romance with a capital R.

When assessing the rest of the field for possible winners look no further than PAMELA ANDERSON and TOMMY LEE, who were 3–1 in the market downstairs when I last took a peek at the bookies' boards. It's hard to imagine so much artistic talent crammed into two human beings. Aren't we blessed to be alive at the same time! I don't know whether you would have had a chance to take Pam's art on board. It's all been good. And what Tommy brings to the drum seat of Motley Crue—well, he hits a tom-tom as though he's killing a wild pig on the toe. And I like it.

This happy duo, having known each other for four days, decided to get hitched on a beach in Mexico. It was a moving ceremony—just two very fit people on the sand, hardly knowing each other, certain of only one thing: that their love would last at least until the next LA earthquake.

Tommy's ex, HEATHER LOCKLEAR, put the mock on the happy couple in a move that can only be described as sour grapes when she blurted out, 'Pam better look out, because Tommy will kill her!' It was only then that I realised Heather had taken over the script writing chores on Melrose Place. I love Heather, I love everything she does in Melrose, and I love her wonderful attempts to bring about world peace by power dressing in short suits and endlessly bleaching her hair. But as far as Tom and Pam and trouble are concerned, so far so good.

But it hasn't been all

I love Heather, I love everything she does in Melrose, and I love her wonderful attempts to bring about world peace by power dressing in short suits and endlessly bleaching her hair.

good news in this year, the Year of Romance. I feel it would be wrong and I would be letting the UN down in this its fiftieth year if I didn't report that everything has not been ticketyboo between the sheets of the world.

There has been a flare-up in that tricky UN hot spot that's LIZ TAYLOR's life. 1995 hasn't been kind to Liz. Sadly, super-star Liz and her tradesman husband LARRY FORTENSKY have decided to split up and seek their own space. Apparently they couldn't find enough space in their forty-room mansion to avoid each other.

It's so hard from this vantage point to get an accurate assessment of what went wrong for Liz and Larry. They set off on life's great voyage with so much hope and the best wishes from the whole film community. And now this marriage, which I believe was made in heaven, has turned out a dud. Larry is a dud just like all the other duds Liz has taken on. Lackers is back driving a water truck on an LA building site and Liz, when last I heard, was making a beeline for

JOHNNIE COCHRANE, the celebrity lawyer who headed up OJ's dream team defence.

In 1995 RICHARD GERE found it difficult to make the hard romantic yards with CINDY CRAWFORD. Now who hasn't admired Richard on the big screen? He is probably the finest actor of a generation apart from our very own AUSSIE JOE BUGNER. (Although to give Aussie Joe his due, he does have more poses and facial expressions than Big Dick.) With Richard's interests in Buddhism and zany activities at the back door I thought he would be natural for supermodel Cindy with her IQ up round the 174–176 mark. But Richard has found it difficult to compete with Cindy's own blossoming movie career. I am not writing them off completely, but the signs do not look good.

And so to my favourite couple and to the winners' list in a very competitive year in this the International Year of Romance. As I open the sealed envelope I believe I will surprise no-one when I announce the Couple of the Year for 1995 to be

Australia's very own MICHAEL HUTCHENCE and the very fabulous PAULA YATES.

Michael is an old-fashioned style of hell-raiser who picked up the baton that OLIVER REED dropped when he went very quiet. Like the Big O, Michael is a bit of a loon—a wild and crazy champ of stupidity who loves putting it about and getting people talking. Paula was born with a gift to entertain. The trouble is that she believes she has to entertain not only Michael and her ex, Bob, but the tabloids, the television, all of Britain and the whole world. Realising that she was born to entertain, it must have been a bit of a shock to discover she has no actual skill at her chosen craft. But she's worked very hard up the fruitier end of the spectrum with the crazy-coloured hair, the wild gear and the stacking on of those extra kilos upstairs with the help of the surgeon's knife. Both have such a sure touch with the international media that you can't help but like them, and they have selected themselves as winners with rumours of wild

flute work hourly by Michael 365 days of the year. According to Paula, no-one on this planet in this day and age is able to tune the trumpet and clear the spit valve at the same time quite like Michael.

THE CALL OF THE CARD

And so let me set the last twelve months out in racing terms so that those who follow the turf will be able to see where I'm coming from. Let us cross over to Flemington and pick up the broadcast of this Year of Romance Cup as they pass the post . . .

. . . And as they salute the judge it's PAULA AND MICHAEL bagging the fruit platter, with an enormous amount of daylight second . . .

Next over the line are the fast-finishing PAM AND TOMMY, who have their feet right on the till probably one run short of their best.

We'll let the camera decide the issue for third between, firstly, this year's pacemakers BOB AND BLANCHE—a marvellous effort from two old stayers who just died on their run—and secondly, BRUCE AND DEMI, who looked a winning chance at the top of the straight. They caught the eye as they paraded in the mounting enclosure before the off. They wilted when Demi produced the persuader at the top of the straight. Bruce just couldn't go on.

Next in are LISA MARIE AND MICHAEL, the big improvers of this year's field, blocked for a run by the tiring BOB AND BLANCHE, who fell into their lap.

Then locked in a steamy embrace are MELANIE GRIFFITHS and ANTONIO BANDERAS, who could improve rapidly in next year's Romance Cup if they would only concentrate on racing. They are deadset screaming out for further—plugging on RICHARD AND CINDY, next in HUGH AND LIZ, followed by DANNII AND JULIAN. The class told they would be better off at the provincials.

Then LIZ TAYLOR, riderless, runs on when it's all over. She threw the boy as she left the machine. ANDY AND FERGIE struggled in the going, as did CHRIS AND PIXIE.

And last to pull up is the totally bored and exhausted public of the world, bleeding from both nostrils . . .

And so, my very good friends, as we leave the Year of Romance and wonder who we'll be saluting in the winner's enclosure next year, we reflect that 1995, the International Year of Romance, is a year no-one will forget in a hurry. From this glittering occasion here at the Quorn Town Hall we take you back to all studios.

THE JABMASTER-
AN ARTIST ON THE PUNCH

· ·

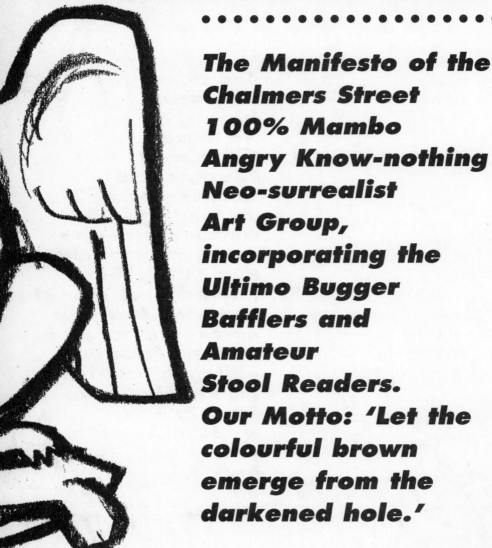

The Manifesto of the Chalmers Street 100% Mambo Angry Know-nothing Neo-surrealist Art Group, incorporating the Ultimo Bugger Bafflers and Amateur Stool Readers. Our Motto: 'Let the colourful brown emerge from the darkened hole.'

THE ARTS NEED MORE PEOPLE PREPARED TO LURCH OUT OF THE SHED AND START SWINGING IN THE NAME OF TRUTH AND BEAUTY. GIVE ME A DOUBLE LARGE ONE AND A LONG ROLLED GREEN ONE AND A PLACE TO PLANT THE FEET AND I WILL HAVE THE WORLD OFF ITS AXIS FOR HOURS.

• •

Our group includes amongst other international supporters the Ubud super-realist Antonio Maria Blanco and the Duke of Kent. We use this manifesto to call on the Catholic Church to canonise Australia's greatest sculptor, Laszlo Toth.

OUR MANIFESTO PROCLAIMS:

1 Laszlo Toth is a saint.

2 Art is dead unless it is on your back or round your buttocks.

3 All gallery art is a sick joke perpetrated on an unsuspecting public by minds away with the big fish on mind-expanding substances not normally available over the counter in this state.

4 René Magritte was a putrid and dangerous joke, overrated when he was alive and totally buggered of meaning now that he's dead. If anyone showed up in this day and age with such cod-ordinary bits of gear like those the big Belgian knocked out every Sunday tucked under the arm asking the curator to 'cop a geek at these,' he or she would be shown the back door pretty swiftly and sent on their way with a boot up the date.

5 The current exhibition touring under the surrealism banner is nothing more than a

• • • •

hastily cobbled together sham. Simply a dud of a show which is traipsing round the nation like a hapless water buffalo stuck in the mud waiting for the safari to arrive with the elephant gun to put it out of its misery. Robert Hughes will have the first shot. Tina Arena the second. They will keep shooting in turn until the beast is dead.

6 Our group does for art what Agent Orange did to Vietnam. We offer a clean start on a blank page and ask you to come armed simply with an HB pencil.

7 We support all artists working in the trying ferro-cement medium armed with claw hammers. We believe these are the only medium and tools left with any shred of credibilty.

8 We maintain surrealism is the product of feeble minds who didn't know who Masaccio was or what he was on about. After all, as Salvador Dali said so lucidly and tellingly all those years ago, 'If Masaccio is so famous how come no-one has ever heard of him?'

9 For a discount on any of the works worn here today ask to see our boy, Theo, at the back.

10 Our group maintains that if any proof of Australia's complete failure as an artistic nation is needed, we merely point out that we have yet to develop a T-bone in club colours.

11 Meat is not murder. It is just flesh off the hoof. Incidentally, we must claim meat is the only medium that can satisfy all tastes.

12 Ignorance about art and meat is what art is all about.

13 100% of our artistic ideas are generated by the 'automatic' writing process. We believe it is the only meaningful form of communication left on the planet. All work seen in today's exhibition has been inspired by the following short spray:

'. . . The Flute, loved the noose and the pants, high the moon samba carpet, the Stanley Swan shirts found the league rugby, the tune was chicken sweet Frilingos.'

(This muse has been formed by cutting up the back page of the Telegraph Mirror into tiny little bits and plucking them out of a Charlotte Hornet's hat on Monday, 19 July.)

14 If in doubt clean the brown from the hole.

This manifesto is signed by PAT CASH (Wimbledon winner) on behalf of the 100% Mambo Angry Know-Nothing Twenty-one.

NB: Laszlo Toth was a man with a vision. His vision was simply that Michelangelo hadn't finished the Pieta. Laszlo was the sort of bloke who could see how this sculpture could be improved simply by belting the foot of Christ with a ballpein hammer, thus highlighting with one stroke the farce that has been the art world since the quattrocentro.
(For further information on Laz see page 196)

FURTHER READING
THE ULTIMATE BUGGER BAFFLERS, THE ONLY AUSTRALIAN ART MOVEMENT WORTH A 100% MAMBO CARPET TILE, a collection of 1,118 essays edited by Ron Barassi and Mario Fenech.
SAINT LASZLO, THE CASE FOR, E. Capon.
100% MAMBO, THE MUSIC AND THE MADNESS, E.H. Gombrich.
THE ART OF THE TROUSER FLUTES AND FLIES, Sir Kenneth Clark.
THE TWO MOONS OF MAITLAND, KNOW-NOTHINGNESS BETWEEN THE WARS, Erwin Panofsky.
THE MOMBASSA STATE OF MIND, Patrick White.
ALL THESE TITLES AVAILABLE THROUGH THE GOLDEN BROWN PRESS.

Vale Shed! Ed, We'll Leave The Motor Running Just In Case We've Got It Wrong

Every sport needs characters. They are the lifeblood of all successful codes. Characters who can do stupid and dangerous things for hours on end and appear to enjoy it. Ed Tinsel was such a sport. He was big for a jockey with a mean streak of uncontrollable brutality which often got him into trouble in the stewards' rooms. But he had his admirers, as Cups King Bart Cummings said at the funeral,

'TINSEL, YEAH WELL . . . THEY BROKE THE MOULD WHEN ED FLOPPED OUT.'

The racing world is in mourning, as last Friday the news came through that Ed 'the Shed' Tinsel had ridden his last great ride and come a gutser on the turn.

Ed's last seven months have been an agony of illness, after he was admitted to Lithgow Hospital collapsing with a complete physical and mental breakdown on Golden Slipper Day in 1988.

Since Christmas Ed has shrugged off the combined effects of glandular fever, viral meningitis, hepatitis B, a dicky ticker, pyloric stenosis, tonsillitis, pulled hammies, a snapped Achilles tendon, groin strain, corked thighs and shingles.

He was on his way home having been discharged last Thursday when tragically he was run over by the hospital courtesy bus as he bent over for a donkey root from a passing kiddie for the first cigarette that the Shed had lit up in eight years. It was the final blow and the Shed passed away at 3.15 that afternoon.

Ed was conceived in the back of a '56 Holden ute on the eve of

125

the Melbourne Cup on Monday, 5 November 1960, not a boot's throw from the finishing post on the Nuriootpa Racecourse. Ed's early years are shrouded in mystery and heartbreak as the Shed, one of sixteen children born to Daph and Bert Ogle, slept eight to a bed and, to coin a phrase, it was luxury if he got one Let's Go Broncos Cheese Ring a week to eat.

He took the name Tinsel from a box of Christmas decorations he happened to pass in a Lowe's Menswear store in Coffs one summer holiday.

THE TINSEL LEGEND BEGAN

The Shed was apprenticed to the Lithgow trainer of yesteryear Fractious Bruce Woodis, but got a lot of rides on the string of horses Roy Slaven used to train in the coal-black hills up around Lithgow.

The Shed's early rides were not memorable, in fact at one stage he held the world record for a losing sequence, throwing the leg over some 5,713 times without saluting the judge.

Roy Slaven never lost his faith in Ed as he never had any trouble making the weight and he just loved hitting horses.

Without doubt, the Shed's career highlight was his ride in the '73 Lithgow Vase. He was the last to turn but came from behind to singlet the opposition on the line on the great staying mare, Princess Pants Off. With his win in the Vase the world was at his feet. In the succeeding years Ed saluted often, combining a mixture of guile, brutality, pulling the head, early starts before the rest of the field got the off, chocking opponents' horses and running them wide, and in particularly hard events he resorted to the Shed special—he simply shot the other horses in transit.

Will we ever see his like again? I doubt it.

All of the Shed's many friends and colleagues and the punting community are asked to gather at St Demi's this Monday for a memorial service which will feature videos of the Shed in action, calls of the Shed's greatest races from Tappy and Rabbits Warren, and the theme of East Enders as a climax. Ed Tinsel is survived by his wife Gladys and his daughters Roxette, Madonna, Kylie, Dannii, Collette, Serena, Tina, Tracy, Dusty, Mandy and Sinead.

VALE SHED

THE PAKISTANI PUNT PROBLEM

Or How the Peshawar Piledriver Pulled In the Pick Four Payout

Cricket is a game that will only survive if it is handled carefully and marketed correctly. Once the public realises there is no difference between a day at the Gabba or the WACA and a night at the Crown Casino or Jupiters on the Gold Coast, club officials will be knocked over in the rush as they struggle to get the 'House Full' signs up before there are complaints in the press about overcrowding.

BETTING AND CRICKET have danced a very attractive rhumba ever since the modern game was conceived by the Big Batting Beard, W.G. Grace, in a backyard in Nottinghamshire at the turn of the century. Gracey knew the code had to offer the fickle English sports follower a lot more than merely the opportunity of seeing eleven cream-clad codgers off in the distance standing around, doing bugger-all for hours on end, while two tearaways ran up and down in the middle on a strip of brown after clocking the six-stitcher

129

radish to all parts of the bright green dial.

THE BEARD REALISED RIGHT FROM THE OFF that punting on when people would be walking in and out from the dressing shed would add to the day out. So along with the pie and sauce, the bucket of chips and the beer in the wobbly cup there was a very real reason to down the blunt instrument, take a day off from the coalface and go.

W.G. knew the financial tickle was the thing that would keep pulling people through the gates forever and not the game itself. He is on record as saying in the *Wisden* of June 1904 that 'Cricket and betting are as natural as buggery and a lot more attractive.' He marvelled at the fact that no-one had put the two into bed before he stumbled out of the rooms screaming, 'I'll never be caught plumb, because I'll simply refuse to walk, so get set with the books on my score!'

SINCE THE BATTING BEARD'S HEYDAY cricket and punting have been merry bedfellows with lots of rowdy high Cs being blown loudly on the slacks sax when the big plonks paid off.

I KNOW FOR A FACT that Don Bradman and Tiger Bill O'Reilly couldn't help themselves when it came to the lure of the satchel swinger shouting the odds. They were at it like rabbits. The habit destroyed both of them. The Tiger v the Don feud which erupted recently and tragically only months ago has its origins in the Don's final duck. Tiger believed Braddles stacked the duck on to clean up with the bagmen. The Big O maintained, until the day he dropped off the twig, that the Don did the donut on purpose because Bradman knew O'Reilly had stacked a packet on the Don, getting the three figures in that final stroll to the strip.

IN MORE RECENT TIMES, who can forget the tremendous elation this nation felt when Rod Marsh and Dennis Lillee took the succulent 500 to 1 about England winning at Headingly in 1980. We wept with joy when the last wicket tumbled which resulted in a shock Pommy win. We grinned with delight when we copped a geek at our Rod and our Den leaving Ladbrokes with the groaning wheelbarrows. By my estimation, these two ambassadors for the code pulled £2.9 million sterling out of the win pool.

THESE DAYS, when it comes to getting set on a game, all the talk is Pakistan and for this we have to thank the genius that still is Sarfraz Narwaz.

SARFRAZ IS A MARVELLOUS HUMAN BEING. He is still able to go Irish off a short run. He can still take apart an attack if a quick ton is required on a snaky, slithering greentop which was trapped without covers in a three-inch downpour overnight. He is the sort of bloke you want to have as a neighbour. If you had a heap of pavers to lay or a washer in a leaky tap that needed changing, or were stuck for a Pluto Pup or a Battered Sav at the Royal Easter Show, or had fallen out of the back of the eighteen-foot aluminium dinghy into the jaws of a great white while fishing for snook off the coast of South Australia, Sarfraz Narwaz would be first out of the blocks with the spirit level, free advice, the wallet or the gun. He is very kind to animals. On tour, he is always on the lookout for a sick bird, a wounded 'roo or a winged platypus that he can nurse back to full health and then donate to a local zoo.

HE FIRST CAME TO MY NOTICE after finishing an eye-catching, be-on-me-next-time fourth in the World's Greatest Bowl-Off at the Gabba some years back. This was a wheeze that Channel 9 came up with as a little lunchtime entertainment in a desperate bid to hold the fickle audience who always switched over to take on board the thoughts of Phil Donahue at the long break. The contest was a six-ball blast-off at one stump with the radar gun used to settle the kilometres-per-hour debate, with your own eyes sorting out the accuracy problem. It was a four-way showdown featuring, from memory, Thommo, D.K. Lillee, the Lion of Lahore, Imran Khan, and the Peshawar Piledriver, Sarfraz Narwaz. It was a very keen betting competition, as all cricket fans love to see a couple of big strike bowlers going off for a fat purse. The Piledriver came into the stink white-hot after a total destruction of the Australian line-up at the MCG days earlier.

HE SAID TO ME IN THE CAR PARK before the off, 'H.G., before you go the plonk take a shufti at my pants. They let you know where I'll finish.' As the four super quicks paraded at the Vulture Street end, I noticed nothing at all amiss with Sarfraz's trousers. They were the regulation creams in which Sarfraz had dressed to the left. As he strolled to the top of the mark for the first ball of the competition, the Piledriver could see I was nonplussed.

HE BENT OVER TO TIE A SHOELACE. His buttocks were five centimetres from my nose. His tweaking finger was on the point. Then I got it. Everything at once, the aroma, the pheromonic communication, the groaning Y-fronts, the sheer strength packed into the buttocks and the four separate brown stains on the back of his pants. That was good enough for me. Off I shot. I got set with a big drink on the TAB and with Fat Cat Ritchie who was swinging the bag at the top of the run. Sarfraz didn't disappoint. Thommo won in a stroll and took home the fruit.

THE PILEDRIVER PLUGGED ON INTO THE FOURTH, exactly as I predicted by the carpet skid marks on the creams. I was a winner with a reason to live because I had a code to love. Now the traditionalist view of betting on cricket sees only two axes of action: how many and when. Establishment books are framed on how many Mark Waugh will make, and when and how he will get out, and on how many Bloodnut 'Billy the Kid' Craig McDermott will snare and at what cost.

SURE, YOU CAN DABBLE in how many runs will be notched before lunch, between lunch and tea and for the last session on the day's play, who opens the bowling, which end, and how many wickets before the tea break, etc, etc. But you can be entertained fiddling about at the edges for only so long. THE AMAZING GENIUS OF THE NARWAZ punting revolution was that it came up with what are known beyond the pickets as the FULL CREAM EXOTICS. These are the equivalent of the trifectas, superfectas and pick fours for people familiar with going the plonk on the racetrack.

THEN I GOT IT. EVERYTHING AT ONCE, THE AROMA, THE PHEROMONIC COMMUNICATION, THE GROANING Y-FRONTS, THE SHEER STRENGTH PACKED INTO THE BUTTOCKS AND THE FOUR SEPARATE BROWN STAINS ON THE BACK OF HIS PANTS.

FOR INSTANCE, when Dean Jones was part of this nation's first eleven there was always a very keen betting comp on Dean's cruet-clutching work. Dean, as cricket-lovers will recall, loved to have a fiddle between each delivery. He liked to settle the trouser trumpet down after ducking away from a vicious bouncer steaming head high off a cruel length. Jonesy was rarely satisfied with the way the cruets were hanging. There was always work to be done in the pants before the next rocket attack with the new ball. Whenever Dean strolled out, bets were taken on how often he would fiddle between each delivery, how many gropes he'd make in an over, how many clutches he'd have at trousers in an innings. Plus most turf agents would let you on stabbing percentages, as in gropes per hundred runs scored, gropes per innings over the last five Test series against the old foe, highest gropes per ground and so on. The Sarfraz Tabaret-style punt revolution was a breath of fresh air. It was as refreshing as the Doctor on a hot February day at the WACA. The establishment hated it because they could not see the card or frame the odds in that wristy subcontinental way that is Sarfraz Narwaz.

EXOTICS OVER THE YEARS have included how often Merv Hughes's tongue would leave the throat and which holes it would be poked into. How often Ian Chappell would drop the F-word in a season of commentary. How many chews per delivery Mark Taylor would cough up on the Hubba Bubba at first slip per over per session per series. Make no mistake, the possib ilities were limited only by the financial and mathematical dimensions of Sarfraz's very active mind and his ever-growing wallet.

BUT THE GREATEST INNOVATION from the Peshawar Piledriver in the betting caper was the removal of uncertainty from any of these wagers. As you can appreciate, a fun day at the Adelaide Oval, the prettiest cricket ground in the world, can be ruined if there are no big collects after the final delivery of the day. As Sarfraz bellowed at me as we left the bookies with our winnings after a Dean Jones—MCG—hundred, 'H.G., why leave any of this to chance? It is so easy to bake a cake when everyone wants to help you make the fruit pie.' I still haven't, after several decades trying, unravelled the full meaning

134

of this ancient piece of Hindu philosophy, but I can get behind his mantra.

MY VERY GOOD FRIENDS, as nearly as I can tell from an extensive scrut of the *Wisden* files, not a ball in cricket at a Test or state or district level has been bowled in the last three decades without there being something on it. The outcome, whether it was tonked for six over the point boundary, whether it was knocked for four past the diving square leg, whether it trapped a top order big name plumb, or whether it was merely a dot ball, was known well in advance. And someone, somewhere, made a killing.

THE GIFT TO CRICKET from Sarfraz Narwaz was to take the pain of punting away and just leave winners grinning.

And for those who doubt Sarfraz's skill: it is fairly easy to cook a Shane Warne hat-trick against the Poms at the MCG, but what are the odds of Dominic Cork snaring the same against the West Indies at Old Trafford? Ooh la la! I have my hat and my pants off to the genius that is the Piledriver from Peshawar, Sarfraz Narwaz.

FOREIGN! ...

Cars—love them, hate them. How can you do without them? The eternal truth about Australian automotive life since the last really big show has been fought out in used car lots, on the roads, at Mount Panorama, down suburban driveways and in the sheds of this nation. It is a stink between the Ford and Holden. Never mind what the model or the capacity are, whether ute, panel van, V8, family sedan, wagon, recreational vehicle or the one tonner, the big two were each year slugging it out toe to toe, mano y mano. These days we have to think foreign. Is it too much, too soon?

A MEETING IN DESERT HEAT

My very good friends, let me set the scene. I first met Erik Carlsson, the super-swift Swede, trying to fashion a water pump from a Patra orange juice bottle for a Saab 9000 bogged up to its axles in sand on the outskirts of Abû Zabad, deep in the heart of Sudan, during the Paris-Dakar Flit of 1971.

136

With Features We Hardly Know What To Do With

PARKED STARWAGON

Erik was not the only competitor in trouble that year. My Team Slanel entry, a Kingswood ute sponsored by the Slaven Nelson Group of Companies, sank down to its rims after clipping a granite boulder which ripped the radiator clean away just before I encountered the big E and his water pump problem. It was the end of the Slanel challenge. I had been travelling for the last three days across the darkening desert with my ignition coil shot, the gearbox full of sand, a blown head gasket, a dodgy diff and the car spewing smoke from the tailpipe.

The Kingswood was buggered. I was history. I was prepared, for the first time in thirty years of competing in the Flit, to powder and chuck in the towel.

I knew Erik was somewhere up in front of me leading the charge and I was certain I was running second. But I hadn't seen a fellow competitor or Paris-Dakar official since leaving El Khârga in Egypt five days before. **Erik was setting the pace up front and the Kingswood ute was keeping him honest. The rest of the field was strung out between Abû Zabad and Alexandria**, apart from some poor buggers who had turned right on the outskirts of Alexandria instead of left and were now hopelessly out of touch with the leaders as they struggled across Saudi Arabia towards Teheran.

Incidentally, there are no roads in this part of Africa as we in Australia understand the concept. In the Sudan you drive on guts and intuition, blasting away, letting the chips fall where they may, hoping like hell that the car will be in one piece at the end of each stage.

As the Kingswood ground to a halt I recognised Erik the Red as I came up over a desert dune and plunged down the far side absolutely unsighted on my way to disaster. The sandstorm that had been howling across the Sahara from Tunisia for three days engulfing the entire Flit field, forcing competitors to drive blind and bump their way across the desert, lifted for a moment and in the midday twilight gloom I saw Erik at work on the Saab some three kilometres straight in front.

The forty-degree air around me seemed to cool as I saw the big man quietly going about his handiwork with a pair of tin snips, a set of allen keys, a half a dozen Sidchrome sockets and a supersized pair of Stillsons.

All I could see of Erik as I approached the Saab was a pair of buttocks, the shorts round the ankles, the back door pointing north in a desperate bid to keep cool under that blazing, strength-sapping desert sun. There was absolutely no mistaking the big man bum-on, even from three kilometres away, as he fiddled about under the bonnet with the tool trying to loosen a couple of stuck nuts.

As I approached the Saab, Erik, without looking up, greeted me, saying, 'H.G., what kept you? I expected you here twenty minutes ago. Now hold this spark plug in the slot while I give it a bash with the ballpein hammer.'

Eventually, after a day of trial and error, inspirational automotive engineering and a continual rewriting of the Saab works manual, Erik fixed the Patra orange juice bottle to the motor. It made a passable water pump and got the Saabmobile moving. We limped into Abû Zabad. Erik, rather than pressing on, decided to wait until officials showed up to clock him in and flag him off for the next stage.

We spent three days waiting for a sign that the rally was still on. And it was only after Richard Carleton and a 60 Minutes crew tracked us down in Abû Zabad that we realised we were still in the race, but it took another twenty-seven days for any official to catch up with us.

AN OASIS FOR THE BODY AND MIND

Abû Zabad is a tiny desert watering hole nestled round a thirst-quenching oasis 600 kilometres southwest of Khartoum. The spot is a little off the normal P-D rally run, but '71 was an unusual year. It was a killer year. It was a black year for the event. It was the year only three teams finished: Erik Carlsson, Team Slanel and the *Just Kidding* team, with Kimberly the Poet at the levers of the Ford F100 and Sam Newman poring over the maps in the navigator's chair. Nissan lost twelve of its crew of fifteen. A driver, a navigator and support vehicle were found several years later, just a bundle of bones being bleached in the desert sun.

The desert makes you mad and in '71 it sent drivers loony. It can make you see things, it can turn sane minds into fruitcakes. **I passed a French team a day before I ran into Erik's Saab, driven out of their minds after drinking the oil from their sump. I saw them dancing nude, quite happily to a certain death, whirling like dervishes across the desert to the driving, frenetic sound of the Ted Mulry Gang classic 'Jump in My Car'.**

● ● ●

The automotive desert roadshow was routed through this small desert outpost because of severe political disturbances along the more conventional route.

One of the chief delights of Abû Zabad was found in the tiny back streets just off the main drag, past the post office and before you reach the petrol station. It's just a little nook which serves the finest prawn and salad roll in Africa. The spot is called 'The S.D.C. Boon'. The Boon is run by a couple of cricket-mad Sudanese brothers, Theo and Thorsteen Nutte, who love the work of the Tasmanian super bat. The Boon is a must-stop for all crews travelling in that part of Africa. **Many a Flit crew, once they got their feet up in the Boon and their teeth deep into a prawn roll, felt they had arrived**. They forgot where they were going and were wooed to linger longer. They felt the swirl of the ceiling fan and savoured the Eastern delights full of mystic promise and the famous Nutte hospitality and found it just too hard to leave.

Erik and I sat in Stumpy's for three days and talked nothing but cars, passing the long days drawing diagrams on the serviettes of changes we would like to make to the average rally automobile. As we hoed into a couple of prawn rolls, lemon juice and coffee, Erik began by saying, 'It's a funny thing, H.G., but cars love to bludge. They would rather be out back in the shed up on blocks, loafing about on the tool, out of sight, out of mind, than out here working hard, putting in and trying to win. Honest, H.G., cars are lazy, bludging pillows.'

After eight days of intensive discussion in the dark recesses of the Boon, I found myself reassessing my opinion of Erik, who up until this point I had always considered a bit of a clown who probably needed to spend a week or two in the room of mirrors. By the end of that long day's journey into the next fortnight I had him right up there with the great automotive minds of this century, namely Brockie, the team that gave us the Torana GTHO-X, the genius who conceived the Lightburn Zeta, the boffin that did the legwork on the Holden Monaro, and of course the original crew that put the Nissan Cedric together in total secrecy all those years ago in Japan. I had him right up there with the top five. As we waited we became friends. Our friendship is based on cars and food, and I like to think that some of the innovations and style in the current Saab 9000 range are a result of those long desert conversations.

A LONG DIG IN THE BOON PAYS OFF

Since that initial twenty-seven days stranded in the Boon, Erik the Red has brought his ideas and his experimental cars to Australia many, many times. The big bloke follows his ideas from drawing board to showroom floor and has road-tested his crates all over Australia away from the prying eyes of the snooty European automotive press. These trips have paid dividends as the resulting product has won acclaim with the motoring public and hard-to-please automotive critics.

Erik's innovations don't come by sitting out the back in the shed on the tool, thinking of winning the big one. They come in the cauldron of competition.

For example, this new signature model Saab has a sunroof. It's not the most necessary ingredient in a car but it comes from a moment when it mattered to have it.

One afternoon Erik and I were trying to make up time on a special section of the Annual Lithgow/Nuriootpa Dash, Bash and Splash for Cash sponsored by the Slaven Nelson Group of Companies. It's a casual affair, where we invite the world's top 200 rally drivers to line up and go the distance between the two towns without ever letting the boots of the beasts touch bitumen. It's a strictly go-for-it, let-it-all-hang-out style of event. In the '90 Dash, just out of Mildura, Erik decided to get the drop on the rest of the field by taking a short cut down the Murray. **Unfortunately, we got into a tight spot as a flash flood came up just as we had set the cruise control, got the feet up on the dash, baited up the first hook and were on the wait to land a groper or a kilometre of Murray cod**. It was then that we saw the flood, a ten-metre-high wall of brown turgid water just as we navigated a big right-handed. We were too far in to pull out. The water engulfed us. Erik was very cool. He had never been underwater in a car. He wanted to see how the new car would perform in these conditions. The door seals worked a treat. The motor kept turning over. The weather wall controlled the humidity in the cabin. Seat warmers kept us snug as we bumped down the sandy river full of snags, rocks and old car bodies that had been dumped by their owners to bag the insurance payout. Visibility was the only problem. We hadn't a clue where we were going. The genius of working with Erik under pressure is that he is not bothered by anything. He simply pulled out a Swiss army knife and cut a hole in the roof using the can openers. He stood on the passenger's seat, popped his head up above the water line and shouted, 'Hard right, H.G., and give it the gun!'

As the cabin of the car filled with water I took a big gulp of air and flattened the accelerator. The turbo kicked into life and we clawed and crawled our way to the bank with the drop on the rest of the revheads competing in the Dash for Cash.

The sunroof incident illustrates that you have to have total confidence when working with the big E. I often wasn't sure when I first began packing down with him at the automotive coalface whether he was playing with a straight bat or winding me up. He loves to put you in the hot seat and see how you and the machine respond.

Erik caught me out one day with a zany bet, late in '87, as he was working on the prototype for this current signature model. He bet a thousand dollars that he could navigate me from the Carlton post office in Melbourne to St George Leagues Club in Kogarah up the Princes Highway.

I said, 'Erik, don't be an idiot, of course you can. Just give me the cash in used notes before we go.'

'Not so fast, sport,' was Erik's reply. 'I'm going to be in another car and navigate your car using the car phone.'

'A doddle,' I replied.

'But, H.G., you have to do it blindfolded.'

Well, in those crazy days I was game for anything and a thousand dollars—well, it was money for old rope.

Then Erik demanded I drive by numbers. He devised a simple enigma code, ie, one—hard right; two—straight ahead; three—hard left, etc, etc. This system of navigating means that you don't do anything unless you have total confidence in the fellow traveller calling the shots in the following car.

At the beginning, as I drove north up Lygon Street, I was pretty tentative but I soon got the hang of his system. The car responded magnificently, despite being recarpeted with brown Axminster throughout as we progressed up the Hume. And I emerged at the end of the run an entirely new person.

A MEAL RIGHT OFF THE MOTOR

Finally, Erik loves to get on the tooth. The first time I went on a wander with him, we set out from Adelaide, arriving at Wilpena Pound around three in the afternoon. Erik had something to show me and put the car into first gear and drove up St Mary's Peak, the highest mountain in that fantastic area. It was a hair-raising drive up vertical rock faces and it was marvellous to see Erik giving the car that sort of stick. We reached the top breathless and after a large one while we were standing there enchanted by the vast and sweeping view, Erik said casually, 'H.G., what do you fancy—the rack of lamb or the lovely beef, broccoli and five-spice dish?'

I thought hullo, the bloke has finally gone, cracked. This mountain climb has broken him like a twig. But to humour him I said, 'Erik, I'd love the lamb if it comes with mint sauce.'

He said, 'No worries. Stay here, son.'

Then Erik, much to my astonishment, simply walked over, pulled up the bonnet, and from either side of the engine block lifted a couple of Alfoil packets. The rack of lamb was done to the point of perfection, and the mint sauce, ooh la la!

Before we set off on the perilous descent, **Erik set out the menu for the trip home. He pulled out of the esky a dozen tommy ruffs and a lovely piece of sea perch which he threw onto special customised slots on either side of the donk with a garnish of parsley and lemon for a meal which would be done to a turn after the run back to Adelaide**.

Like all Australians I love a good car rally, whether it be a social point-to-point with the golf club, a gymkhana that doubles as a progressive dinner on a Friday night with a New Age men's group, a Bundanoon-to-Bunbury dash for cash to raise money for sick kiddies, or a stiff night-time sprint through the last remaining untouched wilderness areas of the nation knocking over endangered species along the way as part of the World Rally Championship points competition. I love the feeling of the blood rushing, the adrenalin pumping, greeting bleary-eyed officials sick from lack of sleep at the end of a stage in a car that is on its last legs knowing once again you have beaten the clock. I love the fights at the end of the day because the navigator got you onto the mud patch with the

busted windscreen simply by shouting 'half left' instead of 'hard left'.

I love a car that can cut loose for the ordinary person, that can exude authority up front as the field is flagged away and then back up and look good on a family touring holiday. Saab has come up with such a car. The Big E has applied his years of motoring experience to the caper and turned out a cracker with his signature range of Saab 9000s which has his footprints and hips splattered all over it.

And if you're thinking of tackling the Sydney–Darwin bash next year you could do a lot worse than shelling out on the Carlsson and doing the run in a little bit of style. It's a car for you if you want to set the pace, have daylight running second and the other pillows in the caper eating your dust and squealing, as they sink up to the door handles in bulldust, 'By gee, Frank, that team in the Carlsson are doing it in style!'

PARKED STARWAGON

IMAGINE BEING ABLE TO RUN HOME FROM WORK AND HAVE YOUR EVENING MEAL COOKING IN YOUR Y-FRONTS WITH EVERY STEP YOU TAKE. WELL, IT CAN HAPPEN, BECAUSE THIS FANTASTIC FASHION IDEA FROM TOMORROW IS AS CLOSE AS YOUR PANTS TODAY.

FASHION
Has a Future
IF IT STOPS FIDDLING

FASHION FOLLOWERS, a lot of minor players with nothing on their mind except lunch have been banging their Porsche 911s and Nissan NX Coupés into my ute at the traffic lights and yelling out above the roar, 'H.G. what's your secret? Why is The Secret Society such a success?' And you know, off the cuff I don't have the complete answer.

We launched The Secret Society range years ago and I saw myself then as an average Joe running round the fashion paddock with two pieces of bread looking for that elusive piece of cheese. If at the end of the day I left the spring parades with the comforting feeling of a heavier wallet then that was just icing on the cake.

I had seen other Joes and Joannas crying out for value to be put back into the fashion dollar in the form of a shirt for their backs. The rest is history. The Secret Society's three initial winners were, first, the wet look. This was a simple line which enabled the wearer to look good, look smart, look sharp, ie, look wet—even on the hottest day in the centre of the most arid continent on the planet when the humidity plunged to the minus numbers. It was our first strike at the heart

145

of the beast. The second big mover in those early years was the pioneering work we put in on the hair care range of products. I was sick and tired of seeing transplants go horribly wrong on the nation's nightly news programs and tonight shows. There had to be a better way. I launched the Nelson range of summer mop tops which stayed on in the biggest surf. We marketed these attachments with the slogan 'Only you need know it's a Nelson'. We followed this up with the winter range of toupees which would stay on no matter where you packed down in the toughest football competitions in the world. We sold these using the theme, 'She need never know it's a Nelson'. After three years of trading we had snookered 52.5% of the market.

The third cab off the haute couture rank was our work with underpants. You didn't have to be Carla Zampatti to realise that the underpant was the only item of fashion that had remained the same for two generations. The only person who had added anything to the caper was young Warwick Capper when he was the resident pin-up and fashion statement for the ailing shot birds of AFL, the Sydney Swans. Warwick (or Captain Cucumber as he became known to millions of football-mad Australians) had his own ideas about shorts. Quite simply, he brought a touch of show business that had turnstiles clicking over. The field was wide open. We brought out new styles and fabrics, initially working with fluorescent lamé for the larger man, and then from '82 on we began wrapping the wedding tackles in multicoloured plastic. We borrowed a lot of ideas from the work of overseas masters. Certainly our interest in using Australian colours and new local materials such as koala pelts and tanned echidna hides dates from Oscar de la Renta's work during the Bicentennial. Big, bold and beautiful was our cry in underpants.

But by far our best innovation, and one we have been lucky enough to pick up Design Council awards for, has come by pushing the structuralist principles at the centre of fashion a couple of years ago to their logical conclusion: practicality.

In the current post-structural fashion era I have demanded from my team of associates underpants that have a practical use apart from separating the skin from the slacks.

Last year we launched The Secret Society Jockeroo. This is a high-fashion garment aimed at the busy executive of either sex who wants to save time and cook while they exercise. The idea is as simple as the clothes peg. We have stitched into the pant a Kevlar gusset which can capture the body heat generated during exercise and harness it to cook a meal. Imagine sending the big bloke out for a twenty-five-kilometre run and welcoming him home knowing the roast is ready for serving. Imagine working out at home with a Jane Fonda tape, and at the end of the half-hour intensive dishing up a lemon meringue pie from the undies to an astonished family who just happened to drop in for a cup of afternoon tea.

If these are the main interests of the label then it has been the range of accessories that has soaked up the loose change from the punters' pockets. You can now get the all-meat Swatch, a precision instrument that is not only the perfect complement to The Secret Society wet look, Nelson mop tops and the underpant, but is an accurate if alarming chronometer. We are about to launch The Secret Society cosmetic range of toiletries to be marketed under the alluring brand name of Prince Roy Slaveni. But the real answer to the rowdy lunch crowd is that not only do you need the ideas, the concepts and the drive from the back line, you need a dedicated and committed team who can bang out quality merchandise at a realistic price. Heading up Team Nelson is Rampaging Roy Slaven, a deadset genius with the slide rule who often spends weeks at a time in the lukewarm water of a flotation tank. When he bursts out of the damp room, it's often with a complete range of springwear for the fag end of the nineties. Fractious Bruce Woodis is our head cutter who can quite literally make the pinking shears talk. The sales and marketing staff are under the control of the terrible twins of the trade, Mungo 'Chooka' Willessee and Warren 'the Croc' Negus.

BUT LET'S FACE IT

The Secret Society sells itself because the bottom line is that the ordinary punter is prepared to open the wallet and let you have a deep drink if you offer a little exclusivity at a sensible price ● ● ●

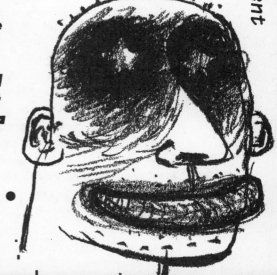

ROY ON THE

Ripping in Rude With a Wet One Pulled On Tight

Roy Slaven, the innovator, brought a little bit of rugby league to the wild, wet world of surfing. He wasn't afraid to go the thump, the dump, the bump and in doing so has changed forever how we see the art of getting the toes right up on the nose and bagging the big Choc Wedge on offer whenever they shout, 'Surf's up!'

A blow-off at the Blowhole

Every year on the January long weekend the Slaven Nelson Group proudly sponsors the Australasian Pro-Am Body Board Championships. The 1992 Talking Tools Slaven Plank Classic was our best-ever competition. It has always been a weekend of hard-core, totally filthy action with the cream of the crew packing down, steaming the pig and ripping the pit to shreds, and January '92 was no exception.

The Group has a policy of putting something back into the community through involvement with big sporting events. We love being involved in a hands-on way with very, very fit young men and women dressed up in colourful rubber gear doing their best to put this country on

148

RAMPAGE

the top of the world sporting heap. The Plank was our first plunge of the toe into the sponsorship pool and it remains special. The 1992 Talking Tools Plank got underway with the heats beginning Friday, 24 January, 6.30 am at the Kiama Blowhole.

The contestants gather on the rim

All the big names from the world tour had gathered with their fancy boards buried under sponsors' decals expecting a top weekend. They were not disappointed. Team Manta was there, as were the BZ wave rebels, the Rip Curl crowd up from Torquay in Victoria, and the Port Macquarie crew, while even Mike Stewart blew into town bringing with him a bunch of big names in from the islands. Locals Wazza, Big Toes, Timbo, Ross Hawke, Mad Dougie, P.T. Hyland, Dave Ballard and Steve 'Bullet' Mackenzie had spent the night three to a bed in a local caravan park and were toey for the gun to go off. Everyone was lured by the attractive purse and trophy on offer.

149

• • • The Slanel Team – the dark brown horse in the Plank

This year the Group sponsored a team to take on the challenge of the Plank. Team Slanel consisted of the old man of the sea, Rampaging Roy Slaven, and the young grommet superstar of tomorrow, Weed Woodis. It was a perfect blend of youth and experience.

Roy acted as captain and was no stranger to the cauldron of competition. The big man had bagged the Plank's lifesize bronze trophy of a nude Elizabeth Taylor plunging into a wicked Waimea wipe-out, and the hefty winner's cheque three times on the trot in the early eighties. He was going round once again, as there was a gaping hole in his life when he hung up the wettie. Everyone knew Roy had one more Plank left in him.

What a contrast in style Roy and Weed represented. Roy had seen it all before and loved every minute of the tour. He loved to throw down the gauntlet, going in hard early and letting the others play catch-up bodyboarding. He always had a gag for the press or a witty line for the nightly TV news crews who always flocked to any showdown that had Roy going round in it.

For young Weed Woodis the Plank was a start. It was the future. The kid was cherry-ripe for the big time, but he was a disaster waiting to happen. The youngster was a stink bomb set to go off when you least expected it, drenching the patio of the shack with an aroma you thought you had left behind after a long chat on the big white telephone in the smallest room of the house. Woodis, or 'the Open Lunchbox' as his mates called him, was a natural bloodnut. His face was covered in weeping pus-filled sores which the doctors could only treat with methylated spirits and silent prayer. But the Box had made a big impact in 1991. He erupted out of the east coast grommet ranks with a great showing for Team Slanel

The youngster was a stink bomb set to go off when you least expected it, drenching the patio of the shack with an aroma you thought you had left behind after a long chat on the big white telephone in the smallest room of the house.

in the Maroubra 1000. In his final prize-clinching ride, the kid got so far back in the barrel that he disappeared up the sewerage treatment works' outflow pipe emerging two and a half hours later covered in Axminster shag pile twenty centimetres deep. Obviously he earnt maximum points and the '1000' trophy in the process.

Weed was a worthy member of the team with his radical drop-knee aerial work and his endless bumbling around out in the line-up on the tooth. Woodis maintained that diet was everything in a big competition. He would often hoe into a couple of large cans of baked beans between sets after gobbling down a humungous length of processed meat he pulled from the front of his shorts before eating a half-dozen pies and a carton of Mars Bar ice creams while waiting for a big set to build. Then he would give it his best with a bit of colourful spit at the end to punctuate a great ride.

The heats of the Plank leave the blow-ins breathless

The early rounds of the Talking Tools Plank were held in ideal conditions at Kiama Blowhole. The setting at the Hole is magnificent, on the edge of the Pacific in that fabulous south-coast holiday and shark-catching nook. A lot of weekend bodyboarders drive straight past the Hole never bothering to check it out but the pros know all about it. The big names rate it as the best and trickiest ride on the circuit.

For the spectator, it's a fantastic spot for a good close-up geek at the action. The Plank organisers take advantage of this and erect scaffolding stands for about fifteen thousand hard-core fans who are right there on top of the action.

There is a little bit of mystery about the Hole. It's an all-air experience. Bodyboarders catch the big Pacific Ocean wheezers just metres from the boil at the Hole's entrance. As the swell forces its way into the vent in the basalt rock, the contestants are catapulted skywards with a hefty spit that splashes the boots of the front fifteen rows of spectators in the stands.

When the Hole goes off, everyone gets a perfect chance to showcase their aerial wares. In competition, Hole-riding bodyboarders are awarded points for height out of the Hole, grace in flight, and quality of splashdown, with extra points for each ride's artistic component, plus everyone scores with the 360s, the twists, the loops, el rollos, the somersaults, etc, etc, etc. Riders have to conquer an initial carpet-laying fear, get past the sickest of jagged outcrops of rock that form the walls of the Hole and find the sky on the spume to win.

A lot of people bag the Hole as unreliable, hard to catch on the spew and too dangerous for a contest. But Talking Tools Plank organisers have never been disappointed, as the Hole has always gone off some time during the January long weekend. If we had wanted a go-round for pillows there is always Bombo Beach.

Once critics and knockers cop a geek at the Hole going off and see a few riders strut their air-wares they quickly change their minds. 1992 was no exception. The media contingent plus the 12,700 fans came away raving after the heats which saw some of the best Blowhole rides ever recorded.

The quality was awesome. When the judges flagged the results from the tower there were bound to be disappointments. P.T. Hyland led the points early with a magnificent airwalk out of the Hole over to the nearby shops for a banana smoothie, a Streets Gaytime, a ham and cheese toasted sandwich, a Kit Kat and a copy of *Tracks* magazine. Ross Hawke ripped the Hole to tatters and had the crowd roaring with delight at his sheer power and height out of it and some wonderful headwork on the descent. Roy and Weed got into the semis with some inspired rides. Roy seemed to have all the time in the world during the heats. On one ride he emerged from the basalt rockface with a live sheep tucked under his arm. Don't ask how he got it up on the wing still bleating.

Roy pulled a stainless steel boning knife mid-walk from the front of his patterned daks. He slaughtered the animal and on the

way down cut off a lamb chop for each of the kids in the grand-stand. Sheer magic.

The semis sort the stangers from the stayers

Unfortunately the Kiama Blowhole went right off after the heats. The morning of the finals dawned with the Pacific Ocean a carpet. The organisers' and contestants' faces were long and glum. The Plank tour director, Fractious Bruce Woodis—Weed's dad—went for a burn in both directions and came back with wonderful news. The Back Door was catching a freakish nor'east swell which was wrap-ping round Mullet Point and grunting green right through the Door. Everyone loved surfing the Back Door. It is a gut-tearing break sandwiched between the Illawarra Abattoir Slaughteryards and the South Coast Treatment Works. When it gets on the poke the Door throws up a big crunching wave onto a small reef just metres from the sand. As it hits high tide, this fantastic shorebreak doubles up on a groyne that provides a breakwater for the local boat ramp. When it goes off it is gnarly. The pits are pitch black. There is not one bodyboarder who doesn't love to feel it smack them between the eyes.

When the Plank caravan of Kombis, Datsun Homer vans, Slanel Mussolinis and Kingswood utes pulled up on the beach the swell was two and a half metres and rising. The waves were grunting through with just a hint of lash and the hardcore that was sure to see a few of the field end up in the back of an ambulance before the 1992 Plank was concluded.

The semis began, Roy taking on Ross Hawke and Weed in against P.T. Hyland. What a contest with all four riders matching it wave after wave! No-one wanted the action to stop and when the siren blew, marking the end of the semis, everyone on the beach agreed it was a pity that the trophy and purse could not be cut

four ways. Adding up the scoresheets, the judges flagged that a point separated all four riders. It was a little bit of violence that got Roy home. The big bloke planted a Liverpool kiss on his opponent as he struggled towards the priority buoy. Roy then applied the Christmas handshake as a semi-conscious Ross Hawke took off on a perfect left. With the squirrel grip strangling his concentration Roscoe went over the falls and flicked Roy into a perfect position for a barrel lasting, conservatively, thirty-four seconds.

When the judges saw that little bit of sauce on the sand it broke the spell and Roy was home by half a point. In the other semi, when push came to shove at the business end P.T. Hyland didn't allow for the Door slamming on him. Just when he looked set to consign Weed to the handbag of history P.T. was snuffed out as the Door closed. He was gone. The Door can be a great leveller. When only Weed emerged from the soup the judges had no choice but to give it to the kid. Mercifully we had the Red Cross backhoe on hand to dig P.T. out at low tide.

The final – two against the tide

The Talking Tools Plank final was slated for 2.00 pm on Australia Day. The organisers were lucky enough to have Joan Collins on hand for a short speech about the meaning of the day and what it is like to be Australian. As Joanie wound up her spray and put the frock back on the starting siren blew. Roy and Weed faced the starters.

The Plank was going to be decided where it mattered, where the surf met the turf in superb conditions. The crowd were on the edge of their seats in anticipation of something very, very special. As they waited for the off you sensed that Roy had saved something extra for his team-mate Weed. It was going to be one of those classic confrontations. Age versus youth, experience versus enthusiasm—all the big questions were going to be answered. For the final the organisers included a special extra feature in the judging. There was to be input from the crowd using the Slanel Applause-o-meter. The outcome was decided with the five judges awarding their points with an extra two points going to the surfer who was able to get the higher reading on the Applause-o-meter.

The smart money among the punters had Roy as the underdog. The semi-final against Hawke had cost Roy. You wouldn't know it looking at him but Roy was hurting inside. The late mail in the ring suggested that it was going to be hard for Roy to bag the Plank with a broken leg, with the groin pulled completely off the bone and with the wedding tackle wrapped in plaster due to a freak accident in the semi. Still, bodyboarding is a funny thing and Roy had proved his knockers wrong so many times in the past.

he was able to serve himself a three-course meal featuring soup of the day, spring rolls and goat's offal paté for entrée, and a main course of Peking duck à l'orange and steamed vegetables

Weed took to the water as Roy pulled on his wet one. You could see the agony in Roy's face as he tried to reef the suit over the night tool area. The Box knew he had to do something very special early in the final to impress the judges and get them ticking the Weed slot on the scoresheet. He knew, at the Door, that he had one real shot to impress. He took off on what turned out to be the wave of the day. A long green wall that had 'be careful sport or you'll get your head stoved in' written all over it.

But Weed had an idea. Well, it was half an idea. He took off and went for it. As he burst out of the first section, he set up a card table on the front of his Manta board, followed by a couple of folding chairs. As he cruised off the bottom with a big turn, he got caught deep beautifully in the tube where he was able to serve himself a three-course meal featuring soup of the day, spring rolls and goat's offal paté for entrée, and a main course of Peking duck à l'orange and steamed vegetables. All this was dished up hot from a solar oven Weed had built into the back of the board.

Then, as the crystal cylinder closed out and spewed Weed towards the shore, he cracked an el rollo off the top of the collapsing section, packed away the lunch gear and stepped onto the beach consuming a sizeable piece of passionfruit sponge while serving coffee and after-dinner mints to the judges. The crowd went wild. The Applause-o-meter went into the red and stayed there for five minutes forty-seven seconds. Weed's army, who were there to see the Lunchbox go round, dropped their pants in salute and the sound of the shorts hitting the ankles was music to Weed's ears and deafened the beach. The kid had arrived. Woodis had already cashed the winner's cheque. But the crowd, delirious with excitement, had forgotten the other finalist.

The Plank was not over yet. Roy was still on the beach. Roy knew the judges could be swayed. Roy had seen Weed's effort and knew his reply had to be good. To rub salt into the wound, Rampaging threw away his Super Special, Custom Built Roy Slaven Signature Model Morey Mach 9.9—the bodyboard that goes with the space shuttle astronauts into outer space just on the off chance they find a wave out there. The discarded board was souvenired by a young kiddie.

Roy grabbed a lid off a nearby esky. The esky was owned by the Talking Beard, Derryn Hinch, who loves the bodyboard caper and happened to be on hand with lovely wife Jackie having a seaside picnic. Roy said as he paddled out to do battle with the Weed, 'Cop a geek at this, Beardie and hang onto your toupee and face fuzz, son!'

Roy let it rip. He caught a great green monster just as the siren went. He got into a drop-knee position then set himself for the barrel. He disappeared from view completely covered up in the crystal cylinder. While hidden away, he reached down into the gusset of his boardshorts and produced a box of matches. The crowd held their breath. Roy torched his hair and emerged from the barrel going off like a Roman candle. When the embers faded upstairs Roy lit up his ockanuis downstairs, pulled off a 360 vertically and left the foamie bleeding on the shore. He wasn't done yet. He let one go from his own back door, lit it up with a match and with an enormous bang took off. Roy erupted from the wave Polaris missile-style and landed back on the beach in front of the judges' tower as naked as the day he was born with the sloop pointing north.

The crowd was stunned silent, not believing what their eyes had seen. The judges were transfixed. One swallowed his Bic biro and had to be rushed to intensive care at the nearby hospital. The Beard broke the spell by whispering from the grassy knoll, 'Nice one, Roy. Can I have my esky lid back now?' Everyone went berserk. The Applause-o-meter went up through green, blue, yellow and into the red and then the roar was so great that the meter simply broke, unable to cope with the strain.

For Roy there was no real surprise as class will always out. He made a beautiful moving speech as he accepted the winner's cheque. He thanked everyone for coming. Thanked the Beard for the loan of the lid. Thanked Joan for explaining what Australia Day meant. He finished his ninety-minute speech telling the crowd they would be idiots to themselves if they didn't hoe into the free beer the organisers had laid on.

Then suddenly the big man was gone.

ROY WAS LAST SEEN disappearing with Joanie into the back seat of the Team Slanel Cedric. As people made their way home from the Plank everyone realised that on that long hot weekend surfing was the winner and out in the water as the sun set there were thousands of kiddies laying waste to the Door doing the things with card tables, a box of matches and their own hair they had seen their heroes do only moments before.

TREVOR 'THE AXE' GILLMEISTER is a man who loves the league. He is the last of the old-fashioned style second rowers who hit them so that they stay hit. From the Lithgow Shamrocks school Trev understands rule one of league: 'Trevor, they can't run without their legs but . . . Trevor, are you listening? . . . Trevor, they don't know where to run without their heads.'

TREVOR ON THE TILES: Chock-a-block Full Of the Angry Pills

Whenever Roy and I travel to a top Quit for Life league clash around Asia, whenever we bob in at a club pie night, whenever we compere a fund-raising underpants parade featuring first grade players we are always asked, 'How does the Axe get chock-a-block full of the angry pills?'

IT IS NOT EASY.

BUT I HAD NO IDEA of just how hard it is to fill the Axe with the angry pills until attending the Broncos versus Sydney Parrots (formerly the Balmain Tigers) clash at ANZ Stadium. You will all remember this game. It was a Friday night fixture in which the Parrots put up a tremendous defensive effort to hold the Broncos to a mere fifty points.

BEFORE THE OFF supercoach Bennett allowed Roy and myself to go with the Brick with Eyes on the Players' Patrol which rounds up all the Broncos and takes them to the team meeting at Bennie's place before they tog up for the game.

THE BRICK, Roy and I collected the Clip Clop Club, Prune and Cumquat Walters, and Three Knees Hancock—arguably pound for pound the strongest man in Asia—without any problems. But when we got to the Axe's place the trouble began.

WE FOUND THE AXE flat on his back in bed looking like a cardboard

cut-out you find advertising a Let's Go Broncos Cheese Ring at the local deli rather than the competition's leading second rower. The poor bugger couldn't get out of bed. Roy went the squirrel grip which usually works on a snoozing player. No response.

THE BRICK rolled in wondering what was holding us up and said, 'Bugger it. The Axe has forgotten to take his angry pills.'

HE DASHED BACK TO THE BUS for a wide-mouthed funnel and a spade. At the same time Three Knees wheeled in from the back shed a forty-four gallon drum marked 'DANGER' in bright red letters—under a skull and crossbones were stencilled the words 'ANGRY PILLS—THE AXE ONLY'. The Brick shoved the funnel into the Axe's mouth and began loading the pills in a spade-full at a time.

THE HARDEST PART about filling the Axe is getting the pills past the groin. It has only been in recent years that a swift, safe technique has been devised by the Broncos brains trust. The Brick and Three Knees simply hold one leg each and as every pill goes in the cake-hole Prune and Cumquat exert a downward pressure on the Axe's bed flute, much in the manner of playing an old-fashioned one-armed bandit poker machine.

ONE TUG and the pill goes into the left leg, two tugs the right leg, three tugs into the left arm and so on. It takes the best part of three hours to fill the Axe but it's worth every minute as the results are on the scoreboard.

Supercoach Bennett has never said a word about this in public but the reason is that no-one, not any body, from Rugby League Week, Big League, the Courier Mail or 'Grandstand', has ever bothered to ask him.

TWO BOOFHEADS
Bagging a Bet, a Bludge, a Beaujolais, and Burbling on About Why the Melbourne Cup is Our Finest Treasure

• •

There is nothing I like more than getting out and about on course at springtime. The roses, the lawns, the fashions, the scent of winning, the big wedges of notes stuffed casually into pants make the trip trackside for the big one a tip-top treat. It's foolish to say that everyone can win a big lick every time they stroll past the TAB, the tote, the local SP or the bookies' stand, but it is true that they're winners simply because they were there. They took part and had a red-hot go.

SWALLOW YOUR SANITY WHEN THE STARTER LETS THEM GO

Wherever we go in the world, as soon as it's known that we're Australians foreigners of all persuasions bellow at us, 'Roy, H.G., the stump-jump plough, the Jindivik pilotless aircraft, rust-free wheat, Sir Mark Oliphant, Athol Guy, *Australia's Most Wanted*, the tragedy of Robin Gibb, over-the-horizon radar, "Morningtown Ride", the Big Merino, Our Livvy, Caddie, Boonie, Fra-a-ase, Sheeds and the Melbourne Cup!'

This is an extensive, honest and telling list of Australia's greatest features but it is the Cup that towers above all our achievements and famous personalities in the minds of our international supporters. It is quite impossible to exaggerate the importance of the Melbourne Cup to all us Asians and therefore to Australia itself.

While nine times out of ten the race is cod-ordinary, drawing a mediocre field of

stayers all on the verge of screaming for the bullet to end their waking, walking and racing misery, it is the metaworld, the universe that surrounds the Cup, that has the world stopping, clutching its heart, going the grope in the wallet and swallowing its sanity for those three minutes and twenty seconds of equine madness.

When discussing what the Cup means to this nation it is wise to reflect at the top of a spray that there are very few events anywhere in the history of time that remain scorched into our memories forever.

For instance, who will ever forget John Fahey's jump for Olympic gold at Monte Carlo when IOC boss 'Juano' bellowed 'SIDEY!' to a hushed world all those months ago?

Who can forget Peter Brock conquering the mountain in 1978 with three tyres shredded to smithereens and a donk under the Holden that could not pull your hat off?

conquering the mountain in 1978 with three tyres shredded to smithereens

Who will ever forget that fabulous afternoon when Lethal Leigh Matthews smashed the point post at Princess Park and called for the trainers to run on and pull a railway sleeper-sized splinter out of his date?

Who can forget Royce Simmons, playing the league for the NSW Blues, being knocked unconscious in the opening minute of match two in 1989? Royce was pronounced clinically dead by the then AMA President, Bruce Shepherd, before putting in a blinder and bagging all the media Man of the Match awards in a game that everyone can recall but him.

Who can forget where they were, what they were wearing and who they were with when the news broke that you could buy a skinful from Bottle-O Jeff Kennett, Parliament House, Spring Street, Melbourne?

This nation remembers, as though it were only yesterday, the moment when A.B. scored his 10,000th run; when Adriana Xenides turned her millionth letter on *Wheel of Fortune*; when Trevor 'the Cracker' Hohn became a national cricket selector; when JPY released 'Love is in the Air' for the first time; when Don Lane and Bert Newton were joined together by coaxial cable; when Pseudo Echo unleashed their version of 'Funky Town'.

FACTS THAT SCREAM, 'IT'S GREAT!'

Punters and horse lovers, those great moments in our history will live forever. No denying it. But they are merely speed humps in the highway of time when compared to the Great Dividing Range that is the Melbourne Cup. Consider the following facts.

- There has never been a fatal car accident anywhere in Australia during the running of the Cup since 1933.
- Since Federation only three of nine children conceived during the great race have gone on to become prime minister (Gorton, Holt and Whitlam).
- The car 'Professor' Roy Higgins bought immediately after scoring on Red Handed in 1966 was a puce green Zephyr Six and is now owned by W.S. Cox of Plympton Park, South Australia. Mr Cox recently described the car in the Open Road magazine as 'a very, very serviceable unit even after all these years'.
- Only four Cup winners have had to be shot within three days of victory. They were Windbag in 1925, Old Rowley in 1940, Rimfire in 1948 and Comic Court in 1950. Curiously, all four were shot by the same person, a Mr W.S. Cox of Plympton Park, South Australia.
- Balloch, the sire of the 1952 winner, Dalray, was the defendant in a murder trial where it was alleged by the prosecution that the fiery chestnut stallion had kicked to death in cold blood the enigmatic yet cruel trainer Wild 'Nipper' Browning.

(The trial before His Worship Mr F. Meagher was aborted when forensic evidence failed to match the hoofprints on Browning's bloodied remains with those of the accused. Ironically, two weeks after the case against Balloch was thrown out of court the 1952 VRC farrier, Bob 'Two Tools' Connell (who claimed at the trial, 'M'lud, the horse is as guilty as sin'), was charged with Browning's murder after the police examined the boot of his Humber Supersnipe and found two severed horse hocks with the hooves still attached splattered with the dead trainer's blood.)

● ● ●

THE FASHION STAKES FAVOUR THE FORTUNATE

But these are just the bald, undisputed and largely unreported facts that form only part of the Cup's rich tapestry.

You cannot mention the great race without thinking fashion. And when you think clothes your mind naturally goes back to November 1967 when Sonia McMahon outraged the Melbourne establishment by daring to show up in green.

- Who can forget the day Jean Shrimpton blew into the members' enclosure uninvited in 1969, alluringly decked out in an olive green Glad bag bin liner, years before the look became acceptable.
- 1971 was the great nude year when the future Governor-General of Australia Sir John Kerr embarrassed himself, his family and all Asia by getting excited when Rain Lover saluted for the second year on the trot.
- And in 1974 a very enthusiastic crowd removed Prime Minister Gough Whitlam's pants and presented them to the winning jockey, 'Handbrake' Harry White, who had just booted Think Big clear in the shadows of the post. Harry, always short of a good pair of strides, donned the PM's trousers and cut a very attractive figure at the Cup Ball that night. Later, Harry had the daks made into four three-piece suits, one of which survives to this very day.
- Sir James Hardie provided some memorable moments in 1980 showing up in nothing but mince. When the controversial winner Belldale Ball greeted the judge, the urbane and witty Sir James replied post-hooter to persistent enquiries from the SMH's Ava Hubble about his unusual morning suit by simply saying, 'Ava, it's been a fantastic day. I've been fly-blown and blown away.'
- In 1982, the year Gurner's Lane won, the members' car park erupted in a wild brawl when Brian Henderson picked on Brian Naylor because both dared to turn up at Flemington wearing the same toned tie.

When the talk of Cup fashion bobs up over the horizon on the dinner table agenda the talk in big hats cannot be far behind. The Grace Bros girl Deborah Hutton thrilled the fashion world by turning up in 1985 with a scale working model of the Berrima Abattoir strapped to her forehead.

The practical joker Kim Beazley braved the inclement conditions in '89 wearing a reluctant Shane Dye as a hat. Shane only got off Kim's head when VRC stewards insisted the boy come down and throw a leg over the Cup favourite.

Fashion and hats aside, to the modern Asian mind the Melbourne Cup is about sex.

1987 is not only memorable because of Kensei's brilliant win but it was the year advertising guru John Singleton and superstar author Barbara Cartland were found in the hay at the back of Empire Rose's float. The fruity and compromising photos taken by Larry Olsen were confiscated by sympathetic Age journalists drawn to the yellow float by the ruckus and the shocked squeals of delight coming from Empire Rose.

It's a known fact that most Australian celebrities watch the big event from the comfort of their bedrooms. As Ann Sanders remarked recently on the award-winning Simply Living, 'The day is a

measure the success of the Spring Carnival by the amount of washing out on the line at the end of the week

real headache unless I get up early enough to be at the TAB before the queue. Then I like to be back home and between the sheets by 2.00 pm. And if I'm spending the day with a fellow traveller I like to time my run so that the bells are ringing over the last hundred metres.'

The Australian face of American football across Asia, Don Lane, freely admits he has never watched the Cup standing up and like Ann he makes a day of it. Don does it with champagne and a chicken hamper and measures the success of the Spring Carnival by the amount of washing out on the line at the end of the week.

Channel 9 supremo Bruce Gyngell remarked recently to the Age's 'Green Guide', 'The great thing about being back in Australia is you can wear pink silk in your bedroom at midday on at least one day of the year and not be thought of as "a loose minx".'

And so we come to the race itself.

The world is lucky to have access to Channel 10's eighteen-hour coverage of a three-minute event. This coverage so beautifully captures the spirit of the occasion that many Australians believe they have been there. On the crystal bucket at home or live on course, is there anything more attractive than seeing twenty-four small, super-fit people dolled up to the nines in the festive colours climbing aboard a hapless quadruped and thrashing the conveyance to within an inch of its life for a hazardous 3,200 metres while the world points, sniggers, shrieks, gasps and stares with disbelief at the result?

We love it. Asia loves it. The world loves it. And all of us will be there again this year, pouring the contents of our wallets onto some hopeless nag who wouldn't have a chance of winning even if it started now.

This horse is chosen by the tried and true Ken Callander method of slaughtering a recently born Santa Gertrudis bull calf and mincing its liver, flute, spleen, dilly bag and snout before hurling the mixture over the left shoulder at a sun-drenched brick wall and divining the saddle cloth and barrier position of the winner from the droop of the splattered entrails.

Why do we do it? Because this is Australia at its very best. At no other time are we as a nation more productive or more focused or more united than at the moment when the cry from the commentator echoes around the globe, '. . . And they're racing in the 1996 Melbourne Cup.'

The ABC found a lucrative goldmine when they stubbed their toe on the large glistening nugget of the debate format. I was roped in for the dummy run at the Melbourne Comedy Festival and struggled away at the coalface with a blunt pick doing a bit for laughter but getting buried by the cave-in of sex.

HACKING AWAY AT THE ARTISTIC COALFACE SUPPORTING THE GAG

L adies and gentlemen, what a fantastic thrill it is to be here in the aptly named Zsa Zsa Gabor Annexe, formerly the Athenaeum Theatre, debating this topic that laughter is better than sex. After all, no-one in the universe knows more about sex and gags than Zsa Zsa. And the record of the Gabor Annexe speaks for itself on this matter. A quick scrut at the Theatre's history reveals that it's always been a place of gags, gags, gags and more gags and very little sex.

Now if this debate was being held in the fabulously luxurious surrounds of, say, Touch of Class, it could be a mullet of an entirely different complexion.

167

Friends, you have to agree that my fellow team members, Mr Gorton and Ms Clifton, have baked a very attractive and convincing cake for the affirmative side this afternoon. My role in the Gabor is simply to add the icing and then place the strawberry on top of the delicious passionfruit frosting and low-cal cream.

My leader Mr Gorton's specific analysis of the business end of the laffs and sex caper laid the foundation for a big win here this afternoon. Ms Clifton, our number two, delivered a very moving spray based on personal experience. It is not as though we on the affirmative side have not tried the other side of the argument. We have. Some months ago, Ms Clifton drew the short straw and gave it a go. She speaks here today in the Gabor room from that personal experience, gained in that cauldron of life. She knows as you know that it would have been far better if she had kept laughing on that fun-filled night some eight months ago. In fact, if she had kept laughing then she would still be laughing now.

What of our opponents, Messrs Jones, Crabbe and Denton? What, ladies and gentlemen, have the opposition been able to get up so far this afternoon by way of an attack on our case? Well, to put it bluntly—bugger-all. If I characterised them as a bunch of bare buttocks stuck in the burning bed waiting for sex therapist Bettina Arndt to put them out of their misery with the big needle, I could be quite fairly accused of gilding the lily, I could be accused of going soft, of taking a geek at the panel opposite through rose-coloured glasses.

Friends, they have proved what you knew when you walked in here this afternoon and clapped eyes on them camped up here on the planks for the very first time. You knew, as I knew, that they were idiots to themselves for showing up and that they need to go into the room of mirrors out back here in the Athenaeum and have a good hard look at themselves. They are quite simply a bunch of jokes!

But let's humour them for a moment. Let's have a quick geek at their arguments so far.

Mr Jones led off with a spit about Gilbert and Sullivan, Chinese food, personal relations and Elle Macpherson and sat down as soon as things began to get interesting, for the obvious reason that a man who can get aroused talking about Elle is indeed in need of a laugh.

The second speaker, Mr Crabbe, simply tacked the 'kick me I'm stupid' sign to the back of the fancy gear and that's exactly what you did.

Curiously enough, ladies and gentlemen, the Comedy Festival has a number of quality videos, polaroids, ten-by-eights, and a lovely sixteen-millimetre colour film of these three relaxing at home preparing for the big day today, sitting around on the job thinking up ideas. When I first saw the photographic display at the Festival office I cacked myself. I was history. Because our opponents are very funny when they're talking wedding tackles and night tools.

The Comedy Festival organisers were so impressed with the mirth, mayhem and magic that this trio generated with the strides off doing the easy horizontal folk-dancing yards with the sandwich, the cream bun or the chocolate eclair that they asked Messrs Jones, Crabbe and Denton to put on a show nightly at the Shaft Cinema round the corner here in Swanston Street as a separate contribution to the Comedy Festival. The organisers, with an eye on revenge, booked the lads in for shows at 7.00, 7.25, 8.15, 9.05 and 10.15 nightly and late supper shows at 11.00, 12.15 and 1.45 Friday, Saturday and Sunday nights.

But I reveal this, not to score cheap points at the opposite panel's expense, but to emphasise that with the opposition—even when the bed flutes are out and in tune—all we get from them is a very big laugh. My very good friends, in all walks of life laughter is better than sex. The boffins tell us that there is a time and a place for everything but I've found there is always time and a place for a gag but there is not always time or the place for sex.

CASES COUGHED UP FROM THE FILING CABINET

Having said that I want to examine with you some crucial case studies that have bobbed into my surgery over the recent weeks. These are ● ● ●

not atypical consultations by any means. As you can appreciate I am a very busy man. I have not got time to search through my patients' medical records to cook up phony AMA-style arguments based on one or two flimsy happenstances like other medicos I could name.

First cab off the rank is the very sad case of Mr Benny Hill. As we all know Big Ben was a very, very, very funny man. I have heard the terms 'hilarious' and 'riot' used by laugh experts when discussing the Ben Hill oeuvre. Now two weeks ago Mr Hill fell in love. No surprise there. Three days after his big public declaration Ben was admitted to hospital with a massive heart attack. What went on at Benny's place? Ben was obviously a bit out of practice. He had given it a rest for many years. He had left it alone. He had forgotten what goes where. He didn't realise until far too late that he was in way over his head with a younger, more energetic person and hey, presto, suddenly mouth-to-mouth resuscitation is inadequate and the specialists are calling for big electric shocks to get the funny man back on his pins. If Ben had only stayed on the job laugh-wise instead of on the job tool-wise he wouldn't have required the very, very serious medical attention he needed to keep him alive until he finally carked it.

I have always advised my senior patients to laugh more and be involved less in the conga line of the horizontal folk-dancing caper as the years progress. Sure, when you retire you might have a lot of time on your hands and fiddling about does pass the time quickly. But it is a very sad aspect of my work that I am often called out at all hours to rescue a distressed patient from under the recently dear departed. In those cases my patients are pinned to the mattress by the sheer dead weight of their partner.

In football laughter is better than sex. Take the recent baffling case of Hawthorn superstar Dermott Brereton.

The Kid was out for some weeks with what the press were describing as an inflamed hip. These were just blind reports from AFL quacks and club butchers for the media. Dermie, as you would all know, is a very, very fit young man and very, very big as many people here in the Gabor Annexe can verify. Round the clinic he is known as the Trombone and the instrument has been black and blue for weeks. You don't have to be packing the A-grade genius upstairs of Geoffrey Edelsten proportions to realise Dermie's injury is one not normally sustained on the footy field. In fact, I believe it is impossible to sustain his sort of injury playing football unless it is after the match having hijinks in the showers, when the gags come thick and fast until the tears roll down your cheeks. The only sound Dermott remembers before it happened was not the sound of laughter but the sound of his daks on the drop.

POLITICS, PUBLISHING AND PAIN

Let's shift our gaze to the world of politics. What better case to illustrate that laughter is better than sex than the matter of Bill Sneddon.

Bill might still be laughing here with us down the deep end of the Gabor Annexe if on that fateful night he had simply feigned a headache in the 'not tonight, Josephine' style, taken a Panadol, turned on the TV and watched *My Name's McGooley, What's Yours?* and settled back for a few laughs. Unfortunately, none of that happened. It was suddenly too late for the motel staff to call a doctor. They were calling for the undertaker instead.

In publishing laughter is better than sex. I cite *The Face* magazine—a very funny read by all accounts. But it strayed from the straight and narrow and what it knew about best, ie, how to make people laugh while talking pop and fashion, and it got into sex. I refer to the matter of Jason Donovan. *The Face* found out just how dear this mistake could be. It should have stuck to gags and how people look in underwear and

stopped worrying about what people did when they took them off.

Let's move on to the world of finance where obviously it is much better to be laughing than to take your hand off the economic levers for a fiddle or worse.

My example concerns Christopher Skase. Let's be honest, Chris is not a funny bloke, but he tries. Everyone knows the Skase story. The Qintex years were wonderful years when everything went smoothly—the chardonnay was always on tap, the prawns were flown in wrapped in gold foil from Honkers, the board members spent their days lying back on the ottomans with the harem pants on asking their consorts to peel them another grape. The hosties and flight attendants of all persuasions dropped everything to party as soon as the balloon cleared the guttering of the fabulous Pixie and Chris Skase Gold Coast love nook.

Chris was very busy making the big decisions. He was buying Channel 7, taking over MGM, etc, etc. Then November '87 bobbed up on the calendar and Chris for one reason or another began to have a bit of time on his hands. As the ship went down Chris discovered other things in life. For instance, he found out that he was married. Chris and Pixie were always laughing, always seeing the funny side of business deals and the banks' problems. The twosome were always telling gags—not very good gags, but they passed the hours between visits to the lawyers. Then the happy couple took a short trip to Spain which turned into a nightmare. One morning Chris couldn't get out of bed. The doctors were called in. After an extensive examination it was revealed to a breathless world that he had come down with something called 'Spanish Back'.

Spanish Back is very painful. It strikes out of the blue. To coin a phrase Spanish Back 'is no laughing matter'. Of course, in Australia we all know Spanish Back as Shagger's Back.

It's a terrible ailment, Shagger's Back. It can grab you when going for that breathless groan. It can make your life a misery. Chris should have stayed laughing and left the night tools on the inside of the silk pyjamas. However, the recent news from the continental medicos is all good. At last Chris is able to travel. He can take very short plane flights of about one kilometre and occasionally travel in the car. So we should see him back in Australia around July in the year 2015.

LOGIC LAUGHS LAST AND LOUDEST

Now by way of conclusion I want to illuminate a larger issue because if—and I say if—laughter is not better than sex, why are we all sitting here chortling away having the time of our lives in the Gabor Annexe? I have not seen anyone here this afternoon amusing themselves with a book in a plain brown paper wrapper; I have not seen anyone turning the pages of a magazine which is only available at the newsagents to regular customers from under the counter. I have not seen anyone throwing off the cummerbunds and joining a conga line past the Kraft Singles and Jatz with only one thing on their mind hoping to get an attractive partner when the music stops. Quite to the contrary. I have seen only eyes and teeth and heard only laughter.

To make this point completely I ask you to listen with me now for a moment. Ladies and gentlemen, wrap your ears around the sound of this great room. Can you hear the sound of trousers hitting ankles? Can you hear the sound of a zipper being lustily and provocatively unzipped? Can you hear the sound of a condom as it's slipped from hip pocket or handbag? Can you hear anyone on the job Bill Sneddon-style going for a big toot on the bed flute?

Of course you can't, ladies and gentlemen, because quite simply here this afternoon in the Gabor Annexe as elsewhere round the nation everyone believes that laughter is better than sex.

It is this fact, this fact that is staring us in the face, this fact that is screaming at us with its silence, this fact of inactivity on the wedding tackle front that remains the hardest fact for the members of the opposition to ignore. Ladies and gentlemen, when you come to score the big one unfolding here in the Gabor Annexe think of the fact of that silence. And as you mark your card think as well of Benny, Dermie, *The Face*, Big Bill Sneddon, Pixie and Skasey, and mark your card **yes, yes, yes, LAUGHTER IS BETTER THAN SEX.**

TV
COMMERCIALS –
Have They Lost Their Grunt?

lullaby of the fish-men

IN ALL MY MEDIA COMMITMENTS, AT ALL MY BRAINSTORMING SESSIONS FOR NEW PRODUCTS AND AT WHATEVER ADVERTISING FORUMS AND PRODUCT PRESENTATIONS I AM ASKED TO HAVE A SPIT AT BOTH NATIONALLY AND INTERNATIONALLY, I ALWAYS PUT FORWARD THE NAME STUMPY BOON AS THE ACCEPTABLE FACE OF THE FUTURE.

I WAS OUT IN THE SHED LAST WEEKEND, feet up on the deck with a lite handy wondering if all those big boofheaded sports stars clogging up the TV with beer ads are the answer to letting us know there is more of the same down at the local in the walk-in coolroom.

After an hour or two camped in front of the crystal bucket I spat the dummy.

This current spate of mindless drivel that ropes in anyone who has played sport in the last twelve years to promote some brand of tins or other has gone too far. It's a farce, a shemozzle, a joke. In the old days there were just two former greats flogging the brews. They were glimpsed playing golf with big clubs scaring birdies, or breaking clubhouse windows having a go at lawn bowls, or playing darts with a bunch of rowdies, or bobbing up in a boat fishing and catching—surprise, surprise—old boots. Talk about laugh. Talk about product identification. You remember them, the latter day HOGES AND STROP, the Zig and Zag of the eighties, FREDDIE AND TANGLES, MAXIE AND DOUGIE, WALKER AND WALTERS. Is it too long a bow to draw to say that these were the finest exponents of the beer-flogging caper ever? Somehow, I doubt it.

Sure, Max and Doug's supremacy was challenged briefly by that magnificent (if prophetic) 'They said you would never make it' series, with the likes of the GREAT WHITE SHARK getting amongst them on and off the greens and WAYNE GARDNER laying rubber ● ● ●

and belting down beers on a Mediterranean boat. Beautiful blokes doing beautiful things and drinking themselves stupid if they weren't stupid to start with.

Then there were the mission impossible ads. You know the sort of thing—the scoreboard at the MCG shows Australia staring down the barrel of defeat in a one-day fixture. The last two are in. Twenty-two runs are needed from the fiftieth over. Up one end the gormless youth from the Hay Plain playing in his first international and up the other the tubby but wily Tasmanian opener with the drooping mo who has carried the bat. I don't have to go on. In the next sixty seconds Australia wins. The tension is so great and the ad is so wonderfully crafted that everyone deserves a beer . . . no, everyone needs a beer.

But what are we offered today?

The BOB SHEARER putting lesson because the plane is delayed. The GRAEME WOOD mini-series, where an elaborate gag is played on Woody based on his liking for the suicide single at the top of his dig, often resulting in him or his partner scurrying back to the rooms before the beer has had time to get cold. THE WHIT'S big night out where a man and his mates are out on the tear, cutting the rug and painting the town puce. There are cameo appearances from SWAMPY MARSH who just happened to be standing around signing a few autographs, and a host of others who quite frankly should know better.

You can call me old-fashioned if you like, but none of these efforts says to me, 'Do it, H.G. Get down to the pub and put another slab on the tab.' And so last weekend I found myself asking, 'When is the Australian Cricket Board going to bite the bullet and demand that all cricketers go to acting classes and get degrees in drama and fine arts before lurching out of the nets and onto the nation's TV screens?' It's all very well hailing the arrival of the next DON BRADMAN and lauding new stars like JAMIE SIDDONS, DARREN LEHMANN and even RICKY PONTING. I have no doubt about their cricketing skills. But can they cut it when the director calls

176

action? I think we should be told . . . because as sure as my name is H.G. NELSON we are going to see their bonces on the crystal bucket down the business end of the games room sooner or later pushing something at us we don't need.

In conclusion, there is one name missing from this ordinary line-up of talent that I set out mid-spray, one man who has the runs on the board lagerwise, a man who even now holds the record for the number of slabs downed on the Sydney/London leg. He is a man who knows beer and could persuade me. That man is one STUMPY BOON. And who knows, Stumpy may even be able to act.

Get a

Roy Slaven's life is one that I have dedicated my own life to recording. From gifted Lithgow kiddie to a true international sporting champion, Roy's career is unique in Australian sport. But when you add in his business interests, his desire to put something back into this nation and his fund of wisdom on all matters which is only rivalled by the Sadhus of Rajistan, is it any wonder that this bio-pic screams out to be made and quickly?

Dog

My very good friends, 1992 will see a dream come true for all Australians interested in football and art. The green light has been given, with the producer's wallet, for the production of a sixty-three part mini-series based on the life of Rampaging Roy Slaven, simply called **GET A DOG.**

It's a story of a gifted kiddie. An enormously gifted kiddie with big, quick hands and a big, boofy head. But a head that would house one of the finest football brains this country . . . no, as you were . . . one of the finest football brains the *world* has ever produced.

Roy was everything a footballer could want to be—a genius with the boot, apprentice of the year, nationally recognised as a slaughterman, a son every mother would love to call her own, top football caller, successful business identity and world-class football historian who was easily recognised bum-on. Roy simply believed in the traditional, old-fashioned softening-up period before a sustained onslaught of going in hard early. He followed the two most crucial tenets of winning football: one in all in, and win the fight and win the match.

GET A DOG opens with Roy strolling up to school from the little fibro lean-to in the shadow of the Lithgow Abattoirs that he called home. Roy skanks in through the school gates exuding up front the authority that he would later show on the football field. Unfortunately Roy was expelled from the school later that day after his first run-in with authority. Battles with officialdom would dog his career on and off the paddock.

The youngster had to do something while waiting for the steroids to work upstairs and downstairs and he got a start at the employment coalface on the boning table of the Lithgow Abattoirs. As a lad he had a long stroke and didn't mind going in hard for the offal stangers, those bits of the beast that didn't know whether they wanted to stay in or come out.

In episode forty-three we come to Roy's football career—the king of the kids, captain and eventually coach of the mighty Lithgow Shamrocks. This part of the story is so familiar that it needs no retelling here. Suffice to say that **GET A DOG** will climax on that one day in September 1978 where Roy, having put in a best on-ground effort the week before to get the team into the big one, is confined to hospital, having broken his leg in three places after slipping on the soap in the showers while whooping it up post-hooter. His groin is ripped clean from the bone by the season's exertions. He has played all season with a busted jaw, never able to find time to get it set. His heart is on the blink and he is dependent on a life-support system.

History records that in the grand final the Shamrocks

are down by forty-three points at half-time. Their traditional rivals, Orange CYMS, had already drained the first keg in celebration of yet another grand final win. Roy hears the debacle in his hospital bed on the local radio. He throws off the blanket, pulls the leg out of traction, rips the drip from his arm, and clocks an uppity matron who asks, 'Where the hell are you going, sonny jim?' Roy, biting down hard on a copy of *Best Bets* to ease the pain, staggers down to Jubilee Oval dragging the smashed leg after him on a skateboard he pinched from a young Peter Sterling who happened to be in town for the big one. Roy motivated the team with a half-time spray that brought the grandstand to its feet. After his spray, and realising there was no-one else, Roy asked the team quack for a big hit before pulling on the jumper he loved so much.

Roy motivated the team with a half-time spray that brought the grandstand to its feet

Roy runs on for the second half. He plays the best thirty minutes of football anyone has ever had the privilege of seeing. With ten minutes to go the painkiller wears off and Roy begins biting huge hunks of turf out of Jubilee Oval in a desperate bid to lessen the agony. Finally, he staggers off and collapses into a nearby horse trough which doubles as the team's water bucket. Roy is out cold, floating in the trough with a couple of dogs that sought refuge in it from last summer's heat and drowned. The big man was brought round by the cheers of the crowd. The Shamrocks got there with a last-gasp kick from the young kiddie who had run out of the crowd onto the paddock to take Roy's place.

The final tune—a very sweet and merry one for the Shamrock supporters—was 44-43. Roy was fished out of the horse trough and even though he was unconscious he was carried by the supporters up to the Bloodhouse Hotel where he was bought round after round by jubilant team-mates.

● ● ●

GET A DOG is a story so vast and so Australian that only a man of genius like Tim Burton could handle the directorial chores. Tim has the runs on the board in the real-life action drama caper with films like *Batman* and *Beetlejuice*. Maestro Burton wields the directorial baton with such assuredness that critics who have seen the first rushes of *Get a Dog* have had to be sedated and in the case of the *Herald's* film critic rushed to intensive care. Such is the power of Timbo's treatment of Roy's story.

To ensure the football sequences of **GET A DOG** have authority up front and complete veracity we are thrilled to announce that the football adviser on the project is the well-respected Lord Peter Tunks, former captain of the Canterbury-Bankstown Bulldogs Football Club. Tunksie will begin work on the script as soon as he has recovered. Unfortunately, Lord Tunks came down with a nasty back strain while undertaking renovations over at Christopher Skase's Spanish double-brick veneer hacienda.

Roy Slaven will be advising on all meat sequences. Who better? After all, Roy has given his waking hours to the home-slaughtering caper.

As for the music, playmakers, it is not a doddle capturing the sound of the big hits, the joy of a try with a kick to come, the pain of the torn cruciate ligament and the thrill of getting the green and gold for the first time. So we are thrilled to have teamed up for the first time since they last appeared at Sunbury the old firm of Bill Thorpe and Brian 'Gingerman' Cadd to handle this, the most crucial aspect of the project.

GET A DOG has an enormous cast with 315 speaking parts. Among the plums any actor would love to sink the dentures into is the part of Roy's first coach, Grassy Granall. Grassy found Roy booting sugarbags full of steaming-hot manure through the barn doors out back of the Lithgow Abattoirs one autumn lunchtime and saw that the lad had green and gold written all over him. Jack Nicholson has downed the tool to pull on the boots in this pivotal role.

182

Then there is the plum of the piece, Roy's mum, Wilemena. She taught him to go forward round the kitchen table and instilled the

Roy booting sugarbags full of steaming-hot manure through the barn doors

fundamentals of the caper in the youngster: the don't-argue, the Christmas handshake, the traditional softening-up period, how to chime into the backline, the jink, the step, the squirrel grip and, above all, how to lay on a bit of nut.

It's a vast part and only one of Australia's truly great actors could handle the scope, the passion and the desire of Wilemena, so Sigrid Thornton selects herself.

I can assure Sigrid's many fans across the country that the frock stays on at all times and while there are a couple of fruity, blue bits in the script Maestro Burton assures me these will be tastefully executed. Timbo has promised there will be no unsightly shower scenes or short cleaning episodes in which the little maps of Africa resist Sigrid's nimble fingers. It's just pure historical fact and who else can do it like Sigrid.

Then there is the part of Kylie, the soap opera star of the age and the other woman in Roy's life. Kyles was a woman of enormous beauty who held Roy in her thrall for many years trying to persuade the big man to take up cooking and bonsai plant culture instead of the league.

The great Meryl Streep is slated to pack down before the cameras as the all-powerful Kylie.

As for Roy's girlfriends—and let us not shy away from the fact that there have been many over the years—the list of performers engaged reads like a who's who of the caper, as it includes Sophia Loren, Brigitte Bardot, Matron Sloane, the great double act of Joan and Jackie Collins (together on-screen for the first time), Abigail, Rachel Hunter, Kerrie Friend, Linda McGill (who has always wanted to get into the acting caper), Julia Roberts and Zsa Zsa Gabor. All these superstars play the parts of those lucky enough to have been romantically linked on the blind side with Roy.

Finally Rex Mossop, the great league commentator of the era, will be played by Harrison Ford in a bold move casting against type. Theo Nutte, the kiddie who Roy first tackled in the four stone sevens and who subsequently spent his youth in the Lithgow Base Hospital, is played by Julio Iglesias and we take pride in introducing Dermott Brereton to his millions of fans in the crucial part of Chook Raper, the Australian selector.

Get a Dog promises to be a highlight of the television and football year. Don't miss it.

Suffering for your art is a tried and true technique for getting people to notice. The genius of the Fringe Festival Card is that it throws together a lot of painful ideas you wouldn't have a geek at once in the same short space of time so that you can have a shufti at them twice.

The Art in Getting the Tripe Flogged Out of You

• •

GOOD MORNING, EVERYONE, AND WELCOME to this very fabulous occasion, the launch of the Fringe Festival Poster. A special welcome to the Leo Schlink Room here on North Terrace. And thanks for joining us on a day when too much Fringe and too much Fringe Poster will be barely enough.

Today is a day that offers the chance for every South Australian to be a little weird, to wig out, to let it all hang out and go a little crazy.

Let's face it, we all live pretty drab and colourless lives. Lives going nowhere. Lives doing nothing. Lives that are a joke. Lives just waiting for the end. We are all looking for a little bit of excitement, and it's moments of excitement that we have on offer here today in the Schlink.

• • •

185

Ladies and gentlemen, here in the Leo today we are offering the stuff of dreams. And if we get hot, if we get very hot, hopefully we can offer an added bonus—the stuff of nightmares. Mark my words, my very good friends, these Fringe Festival Poster launches are things people remember forever. They are not forgotten in a hurry.

I have not met one South Australian who doesn't remember the launch last year. As you will recall, this time last year Adelaide copped a good hard geek at the future PM, totally buffed, running around this very room doing the honours on the Fringe Festival Poster. A lot of people hadn't seen the current PM nude before. Everyone now agrees he cuts a very attractive figure. Obviously he had the three-piece FJ suit back on when the cameras started whirring. But the early birds copped an eyeful of a totally nude PM on these very planks. Who can forget the day climaxing with Paul Keating singing up a storm at the top of his lungs with the genial MC Bob Downe dueting on 'You're the Top'?

the future PM, totally buffed, with a rolled-up *Advertiser* ablaze at the back door, running around this very room doing the honours on the Fringe Festival Poster

Don't tell me that South Australians can't remember where they were, what they were doing, who they were with and what part of the anatomy they were fiddling with when the news came through that the future PM had made the hard yards in the Fringe Poster caper. Don't tell me that millions upon millions of South Australians across Asia won't remember that moment and in years to come, when their grandkiddies ask, 'Grandma, Grandpa, did anything interesting happen in your life?', then grandparents across this great state will recall with affection and pride the day Paul Keating blew into town and snipped the ribbon and got the Fringe Poster off the ground and loose of the power lines above the guttering. It's only the Fringe that can offer such images with certainty. I know for a fact that Paul's performance here swayed the caucus and swung a lot of votes behind the Keating push for the top job.

To return to the present, ladies and gentlemen, I love the Fringe. I love everything about the Fringe. When my partner, Roy Slaven, and I set up Circus World (that is, THE Circus with a Difference) all those years ago people said it was too fringey to work. People said it would not last a month. How wrong they were. Sure, early on it was tough. It was hard to find a quid in those days to keep the show on the road. We were desperate for a loan just for a tent. We even applied, rather foolishly, to the State Bank of South Australia for a loan of $100 million for a bit of canvas. We understand that this was the only loan the bank ever knocked back. That's how fringey the financial world believed Circus World was then. The State Bank refused to lend us money saying we would go broke within three months. But we're still here and kicking butt, and it's the banks who've gone broke.

Circus World began with a simple show featuring Jeff Kennett and His Trained Mice. This was long before Jeff got the top job in Victoria. You've all seen the act hundreds of times and loved it. Jeff comes out wearing the big, fat pants. Very funny, very funny. Then he lets the mice loose from the trousers. Huge applause, laughs and shrieks of

187

delight all round. Jeff chases them round the tent bashing them with a fence paling. The act climaxes when Jeff pours petrol over the buggers (unleaded, of course) then strikes a match. Mirth all round. Finally Jeff buries the lot with a Massey Ferguson tractor. Every night that Jeff and the mice perform half the crowd is carried out by the St John's Ambulance staff and placed straight into intensive care. And that's just the first act.

Jeff and the mice go over very well in the Lameroo/Pinnaroo area of South Australia where they have always got

the act climaxes when Jeff pours petrol over the buggers (unleaded, of course) then strikes a match

mouse troubles.

In the second half of Circus World, it's all old favourites. Kim Beazley defying death by jumping on a crab off a milk crate. Brutal Bronwyn Bishop bludgeoning a platypus to death with a beehive hairdo—a very moving act and very funny at the same time. Then, after Brutal has weaved her magic, South Australia's own Tim May does a bit of traditional home-style slaughtering work with a few sheep.

We pull big crowds because ordinary people don't give a sticky date about your big international festival blow-ins who come with all the hype, take all the space up at the big end of town, get the best seats on Popeye and quite often deliver bugger-all.

Every year it's the same sort of gear. You can picture the bill now. From Ecuador, the all-Spanish fifteen-hour version of *The Summer of* the Seventeenth Doll set on the Kokoda Trail during the Second World War perfomed by the National Bunraku Theatre of Japan. Direct from the Port Moresby Perspecta—the modern-dress version of Shakespeare's Romeo and Juliet, performed underwater by Vietnamese water puppets. Snorkels and breathing gear included in the price of admission.

Or the Russian version of the opera Einstein on the Beach. Seven and a half hours of a cast screaming for help, stuck in the mud of their own making, screaming for the bullet that will finally put them out of their misery. And for the whole season no-one with the guts to go along with a shotgun and do the job.

You go to these shows because they come with an international reputation of being good. Someone has written them up in the Advertiser saying 'must see', 'not to be missed' and 'kill your relatives for seats'. My very good friends, what a laugh! After five minutes you are bored beyond belief and spend the rest of the night asking why, why did I bother? All the signs were there that it was going to be a dud and you kick yourself over and over again for ignoring them once again.

The average Joe and Joanna want to see something different at an affordable price and this is where the Adelaide Fringe comes in. By way of diversion can I make one political point on behalf of the Fringe concerning the very popular Hellfire Club-type of entertainment. Thank goodness the licensing laws here in Adelaide have put the mockers on the Hellfire Club throwing open its doors for a good whipping of anyone who had the price of admission.

These Hellfire Clubs have become all the rage in the other states and, quite frankly, they are ruining the fringe elsewhere. In the old days you

the Hellfire Club throwing open its doors for a good whipping of anyone who had the price of admission

could string up a consenting adult by the bed flute with fish hooks to the ceiling of a room like the Schlink here. You could drip candle wax all over his wedding tackle, while at the same time

● ● ●

belting the living daylights out of him with a bullwhip while he himself drilled the flute length-wise with a Black & Decker power drill and a three-eighth bit. Everyone bobbed in for a groan wearing skimpy leather gear, and all this was done to the very latest Kylie Minogue dance track. The 'I Should Be So Lucky' type of gear. You called it 'an explosion of wrist'.

You declared it art and toured it to fringe festivals everywhere. You got some racy publicity on the old Hinch TV program. Derryn the Talking Beard loves that sort of work and you charged the public a nice dollar at the door to see the show.

Now even though I do appreciate that it's not everybody's cup of tea entertainment-wise, the Hellfire Club scene has ruined this fringe-earner by offering everyone a place on a Thursday night where they can get all this for free and do it to each other into

MALE BICYCLE

the bargain. They are quiteliterally putting hundreds of our finest young fringe artists out of business. So I thank the powers that be here in the City of Churches for leaving this healthy outlet, this very core of artistic activity, for the fringe to exploit. My surveys reveal that 93.7% of all South Australians are prepared to pay top dollar for a good flogging.

In conclusion, as everyone here knows, Adelaide is the centre of the arts in Australia. No . . . as you were . . . my very good friends, Adelaide is the centre of the arts in Asia. It's the home of Humphrey Bear. The home of *Wheel of Fortune*.

Adelaide was the former home of the multifunction polis—and there is nothing more fringey than an MFP. Adelaide remains the home of the Australian Grand Prix (even more so now that it's gone), the home of the submarine, the home of the grape, the home of Wayne Weidemann.

Wayne, now *there* is a fringe, front and back. Adelaide is the home of the Camry Crows. It's the home of that great Australian firm, Mitsubishi. But towering above all of these great things is that Adelaide is known as the home of the Fringe, the real Fringe, the only Fringe. The Fringe that matters.

Ladies and gentlemen, when we get the Poster into the sky and up above the statue of Colonel Light and on its way, simply follow the Fringe lead and 'Eat Your Heart Out'.

South Australia, stick your nose deep into the trough and have a slurp. And when you have eaten your fill to spewing remember to do as the Heidelberg School always did, and simply let the brown be your palette and pen.

Qantas, our national
carrier, has been on the
wing for seventy-five
years. As the festivities
built up a head of
steam, Captain Alec
Baldwin and his
charming flight
crew asked me to
jot down a few
recollections of
the early days
of flying with
footballers.
They were a
hoot. When you
packed a team on
board an old
Viscount prop
jet you
could only
hang on
and laugh
hoping
that you
would get
there in one
piece. All the
cabin staff
could do
was
ease
the
way.

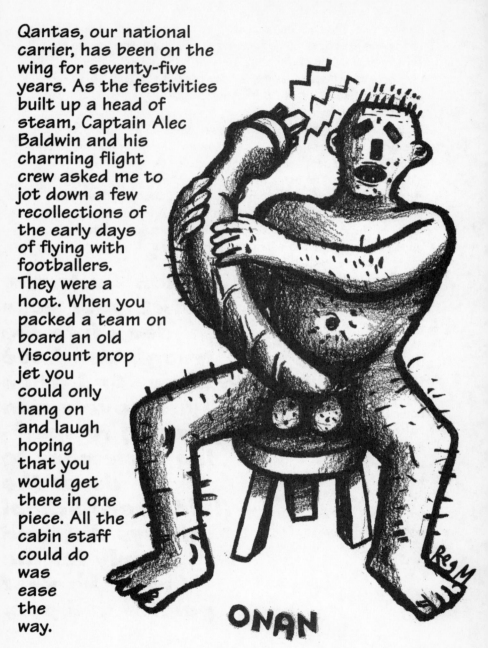

ONAN

On the Rhumba Round the Nation With the Flying Kangaroo, With the Pouch Packed Chock-a-block Full With End-of-Season Revellers

The Flying Kangaroo and sport have danced a very attractive and rowdy rhumba since the Wright Brothers burst out of the shed screaming, 'If this doesn't fix it, let's burn the bugger. Now that could be a lot of fun!'

My own involvement with our national carrier goes back four decades. I was club secretary with the Nuriootpa Tigers throughout those fabulous fifties. It was my lot to organise end-of-season trips for the Tigs.

1958 hadn't been the club's best year. We had snared the cheese in only four matches. But we had blooded a lot of players. The future was looking ticketyboo. Round the Barossa Valley you could smell the golden dawn of a premiership and get a whiff, on the breeze, of silver being slotted into the trophy cabinet in the foyer of the clubhouse.

In '58 I was on a tight travel budget. We raised money throughout the season by selling 47,000 dozen lamingtons. We held a very successful players' fashion parade at the Town Hall in early June. The golf day at the Tanunda Golf Course went off a treat and earned a big lolly for the travel fund. Sure, there was a brouhaha in the clubhouse car park at closing time. But as the police outlined in their report it was just a couple of blow-ins letting off steam about course rules hurting no-one but themselves.

193

Suddenly it was August. We were out of the finals. I was stuck for ideas. Players were bellowing at me in the street, 'H.G., I've packed the bag. Where are we going, sport?' I had twenty-five very fit blokes champing at the bit, plus seven club officials, including the senior coach, trainers, runners and boot studder to transport and entertain for eight days.

I knew nothing about the travel caper. I was starting to get night sweats. The solution came to me in a dream. It was a weirdo pre-psychedelic nightmare.

There was a barbeque. I was playing football while the meat cooked. The chops were yellow and the Shane Warne pink-and-purple snags drifted above the hot-plate. The goals dissolved into a bullseye target.

As I dobbed the Sherrin through the hi-diddle-diddle the smoke from the hotplate was sucked up in the draught of the ball and formed the word 'Qantas'.

Questions teemed in my mind. What could all this mean? I awoke pleasantly relieved knowing who to ring at last. The Qantas people could not have been more helpful. They did the lot. Our mystery tour took the Tigers to Lithgow in New South Wales.

Qantas did not bat an eyelid at our unusual requests. We were able to travel nude. The captain didn't mind removing a few seats for the larger players. We put in the Slip and Slide and Twister mats for fun during the trip. Everyone had a go at flying the plane. That taught us a lot. We knew instantly not to let Fractious Bruce Woodis or Sheddy Tinsel anywhere near the business end after about thirty seconds of terror.

When we were flying over water we were able to fish from the plane. Now that is a thrill. To bag a mullet or a snook from 30,000 feet was a dream come true. As we approached pig territory the captain took the bird down to tree-top level to flush out a heap of porkers. We opened the emergency exits and had a bang at them from the plane. Talk about excitement.

When we got to Lithgow, Qantas had teed up a total week. We toured the coalmines and made cement at Kandos. We spent a day at the small arms factory. After the tour we were able to sample the

194

output and blow off in all directions. We took the ride to the top of Scotsman's Hill and saw a group nine rugby league top-of-the-table clash at Watsford Oval. The Shamrocks shellacked Orange CYMS to the tune of 74 to 4. A very young Roy Slaven was best on the ground for the Shammies. And to top off a great week we got into a stink at the Bloodhouse Hotel. Everyone bagged a bootful of fish and shot a tray-load of pigs. With the group bookings arrangements Qantas was able to transport the loot back to South Australia in the refrigerated section of the plane without charging us excess baggage. As we returned tired but happy to Nuriootpa we were able to gut and cook a couple of pigs on a specially constructed in-flight barbeque.

The Qantas staff organised the lot. By the end of the week I was speechless in admiration. I had my hat and trousers off to them. I still get middle-aged people I barely recognise bumping into me at coaching clinics and pie nights saying, 'H.G., that Lithgow trip with the Tigers was the best thing in my life. It's all been downhill since. Thanks, pal.'

Over the years Qantas has handled all my unusual travel requests with tact, discretion and a completely professional attitude. No matter whether I have been teeing up a trip for footballers, transporting horses or satisfying the tricky needs of overseas superstars, Qantas has always come through because it understands Australians and how Australians like to travel.

LASZLO TOTH –
Genius,
Saint,
Sunday Hacker
or Merely a Joke?

• • • • • • • • • • • • • • • • • • • •

Art, the tourist dollar and racing – they make an attractive three high in anybody's language. Laszlo's tap on the Pieta's toe was the starting point for a literary spray that sorts out for the final time which is the bread and which is the filling.

ON THE TOE IN THE TOTH

I see myself as an average art student running round the gallery circuit with the cheque-book in hand and a warm pen at the ready hoping to see someone go crazy or broke. And if at the end of the day I have seen both then I dash home to the Filofax and mark it down as an absolutely top day. And, gee, in the art world it's so easy to go crazy or broke or both.

Good morning, everyone, and what a thrill it is to be back here once again in the Laszlo Toth Room at the College of Fine Arts on this magnificent occasion—the annual conference of the National Council of Heads of Art and Design Schools.

This morning for me, well . . . it's a dream come true. I am quite simply over the moon because for years I have been saying to arts educators around Australia . . . no, as you were . . . my very good friends, I have been *pleading* with arts educators around the world for someone to bite the bullet and get the big names in the caper away from the teaching coalface, to down the chalk, the pallette and its pencil and lock horns for three big days tackling the big Cs—Contexts, Collaboration and Competition.

And it has given an old Sunday painter specialising in abstract expressionism an enormous thrill to see conference delegates not being afraid to go in hard early, to blast away and let the chips fall where they may and to keep at it even when others going around in the caper have powdered and screamed 'enough'. Of course you can't turn a quid with that abstract gear nowadays, so I've had to give the game away and take up sports commentating.

I think it's very fitting that we should be gathered here in the Toth this morning to contemplate where we are going and where we

have been. I see the next cab off the conference rank is a panel discussion on 'Research and Funding' and I hope in my few moments with you before the first foaming cup of tea and Iced Vo Vo is brought round on the trolley that I can leave you thinking and ready to rip in. It's not my aim this morning to leave you satisfied and sated but to leave you with the knuckles bared and the body clock controls set on fast forward.

By way of booting off I say hats off to the University of New South Wales for declaring this room the Toth room. The Laszlo Toth story, what a story! A story as big as art itself or Queensland, whichever is bigger. I forget these days with the daylight-saving issue clouding the card.

Old Laszlo was a man of enormous vision. He had a simple idea. He basically believed Michelanglo hadn't done enough on his *Pieta*.

Laszlo firmly believed that the Italian maestro had dropped the pill when sculpting the final few yards of the piece. Now as you would all be aware not many critics actually subscribed to Laszlo's theory over the years. Be this as it may, old Lazzers believed that when mad old Mich presented the Madonna and Child to the Pope it was fundamentally an unfinished work. It was a work in progress. Laszlo brooded about this for years outback in the shed that doubled as his studio in Tempe night after lonely night. Then one day Mr Toth thought bugger it . . . bugger it, I'll finish it off for the old man.

One fine autumn day Laszlo hopped aboard a Rome-bound Alitalia 747, got through customs, strolled into the Vatican and belted the foot of Our Lady with a ball pein hammer until the toes dropped off. Laszlo shouted 'Eureka, it's now complete!'

Talk about genius. Talk about insight. Many of the great critics immediately saw that Laszlo had it right. The scales fell from their eyes. Our very own Bob Hughes was persuaded, the great, great Erwin Panofsky had to rewrite his masterwork Studies in

Iconography after he copped a geek at Laszlo's work, and even the critic they simply called the Man, Bernard Berenson, admitted he had been wrong. These three fell over themselves with the brilliance of the Toth addition to the *Pieta*, or to be more accurate, his subtraction. Of course, the world couldn't see the brilliance of the Toth job as overzealous officials superglued the toes back on before the world had a chance to take in the toeless look.

Now having briefly related the Toth story, I was thrilled to see a student of the school of Toth taking a swing at Michelangelo's *David* recently. Curiously enough it was the foot once again. The tool, a hammer. But as soon as the lad had completed the effort you knew immediately it was the School of Toth as nothing was revealed, nothing was added—the blow simply buggered the statue.

So it is no surprise to me to see us gathered here in the Toth with Contexts, Collaboration and Competition on the agenda.

GIVING THE GUGGENHEIM THE GOOSE

Friends, in my capacity as roving cultural adviser to the Guggenheim Foundation I was very happy to touch down in Australia at what we call the business end of the season. I never miss the Festival of the Boot. I caught up with my old mates the Village People at the Rugby League Grand Final last Sunday week, then doubled up and saw Daryl Braithwaite still cutting the rug at the AFL Grand Final on Saturday.

But apart from these pleasures there are three main reasons for being in Australia this week. First and foremost I am here as insurance adviser riding shotgun on the Guggenheim exhibition which has been hurled onto the walls of the NSW Art Gallery. Secondly, I'm to appear before the WA Royal Commission and explain my part in the murky world of high-flying finance that took

● ● ●

199

off like a sky rocket over in the West in the late eighties. And thirdly, I'm available to present some suggestions to the racing clubs of Australia concerning the greatest game of all and how to woo the punters back on course. I thought I might pass the time with you this morning tackling all three.

Ladies and gentlemen, to boot off at the beginning. There is as yet an untold story attached to the 111 canvases from the Guggenheim Museum now on display in Sydney.

When the board of the Guggenheim decided to shut down the HQ for renovations it was only natural that they throw together a touring exhibition to turn a very attractive dollar, given that there were no punters banging on the doors with the wallets out while the renovations were being completed.

To be quite honest, Sydney was not our first destination. To be absolutely frank, Sydney was well down the list of possible venues. We tried to interest the Tate first up. They were chock-a-block full of Constables and as told to me the director had had a gutful of the sort of gear we were assembling.

Next we tried the Prado in Madrid, then the Pompidou Centre in Paris. No luck, no interest, not a bite, not a tickle. All this gear is very passé in Europe at the moment. So much so that the Pompidou didn't bother to ring us back. The National Gallery in Canberra gave us the bird. They correctly saw the show as the cabbage from the collection.

Mercifully we got lucky with Fast Eddie down at the NSW Art Gallery. We were desperate and luckily for us Big Ed elbowed aside an exhibition of CWA tea towels, Holden car parts from the fifties and a retrospective of Kenny Done T-shirts to slip the thing in. There were huge sighs of relief back at the HQ and I make no apologies as we vigorously pulled the beard to get Ed to open up the doors. We simply described a lot of pictures over the ISD phone late at night and then quite deliberately forgot to crate them when we boated out.

Just as an aside, during the last three weeks a lot of people have been bumping into me at traffic lights, buttonholing me in queues at the supermarkets, stabbing the finger into my chest while I've been riding around in lifts, and screaming at me when I've grabbed a seat at the back of the bus, asking in simple language what the renovations to the gallery are going to be and what the old place will look like when the doors are reopened.

Obviously the gutters needed doing. They hadn't been touched since Peg cut the ribbon and declared the joint open all those years ago. And the outside needed a coat of Berger Breeze cobalt blue. That was easy to fix.

But once the news surfaced we were getting out the Black & Decker Workmate we were besieged by brilliant ideas. For instance, Glenn Murcutt swanned in and suggested we put in a bull-nose verandah, knock in a few doors, open up the place to natural light, catch the prevailing breeze and finally hang all the pictures on cor-rugated iron. I could see what he was on about, but you know what a board of trustees are like—they just couldn't see it.

But the real reason for the rennos is that we get so many visitors barrelling in through the front doors, grabbing the lift up to the top and then wailing about the fact they haven't got time to spend thirty seconds in front of every canvas on the way down. These visitors scream, 'H.G., we get gallery fatigue after twenty minutes of staring at a couple of Braques. Isn't there any quicker way to do the place as we have to be at Tiffanys by 11 am, if you don't mind, sport.' So in response to their many, many requests the board has approved a major renovation to the gallery. We are going to add a dual-purpose dual-climate water and ice slide. In summer it's filled with water and then in winter it doubles as a ● ● ●

world-class luge course once the water freezes over. It runs from the top of the building to the car park out back and you can be back on board the tourist bus within three minutes twenty seconds of setting foot inside the place. Patrons who want to see the exhibition in thirty-five seconds as opposed to thirty-five minutes shove off at the top and slide all the way down, taking in the majesty of Peg and Sol's handiwork with the wallet out on the way down, and are then on their way.

But, ladies and gentlemen, first and foremost I must apologise for the cabbage from the Guggenheim collection that is in this current display. I hear a cry from the back of the hall: what about the Kandinski gear which is getting all the talk? . . . Well, they weren't meant to come. They were booked to go over to Ted Kennedy's house for a cocktail fundraiser for Alan Bond and somehow ended up on a plane bound for Mascot. When I opened up one of the big yellow boxes I blanched. I was tight-lipped. Ashen faced. I was in a pickle but I thought bugger it, why should Australia come off second-best in the caper? It was too late by then to get them over to Ted's and once again Bondy's loss is Australia's gain.

Now another common question I'm asked is how did Peggy G. do it? How did she buy a picture a day? How did Peg bag all those pictures at prices that would make you swoon? Peggy always said as she swanned about New York climbing stairs up to the top lofts looking for something new, 'Go in hard early, H.G., and bag a picture before ten in the morning. Get them before those artistic pillows have had a chance to come to and have the first sobering black coffee of the day. H.G., have the ute backed up out the front for a quick getaway and leave the rest of the dorks in the art world playing catch up collecting.' The only other words I heard her say on the caper were on a freezing cold winter's morning as she struggled down with an early Pollock from an eighth-floor loft on West Fifty-

third Street. 'H.G., take a tip. Once you have it, the others will all want it. Who is to know a cabbage from a cauliflower once you've banged the bugger up on the walls and declared it a masterpiece? The rest of the world will want to pay through the nose for it. Now dash over and tell Clement Greenberg to put that in his pipe and smoke it.'

Look, ladies and gentlemen, Peg made mistakes. In the art caper you can get it wrong. So when you go down to Big Ed's this afternoon you be the judge and make us an offer as we're clearing the brussel sprouts out in a once-in-a-lifetime sale. Just ring Edmund after you've picked the duds.

ACT ON THE BACK MEANS LOOT IN THE FOB POCKET

Leaving the vegetable market aside, a substantial spin-off from my trip includes having talks with major department stores like David Jones and Myers about a franchise opportunity selling a line of famous paintings done up in club colours. This has been a big money spinner for the Slaven Nelson Group of Companies overseas. An idea as simple as the fork.

What if, say, you come to Sydney for a high-powered arts chinwag and would like to pick up a souvenir of the trip. You don't want the usual. You need something exotic to impress the folks back home. Imagine being able to duck into DJ's or Grace Bros and bag a *Guernica* in Essendon colours of black and red, or bursting in through the doors after the conference and amazing the family when you pull out of the bag a *Mona Lisa* done up in attractive West Coast Eagles colours of blue and yellow. Or when buying for that favourite uncle who has everything: imagine Uncle Theo's look on that one day in December when he pulls the wrapping paper away to reveal David's *Oath of the Horatii* in the Canterbury-Bankstown Bulldogs colours of blue and white.

Our group, the Slaven Nelson Group, not only has the means to effect these marvellous works but we promise to deliver anywhere in Australia with a twenty-four hour service still wet. If you're interested in exploring these franchise arrangements we have brochures available at morning tea. Just look for them with the Iced Vo Vos.

HAPPINESS IS A NICE WARM SUBPOENA

But look, I didn't come here this morning to bore you witless prattling on about the art world and our problems. I wanted to expand the agenda here and tackle the issues which matter to me personally and I would like to run by you my defence before the Royal Commission into WA affair and discuss two magnificent ideas for getting punters back on track or even back into the galleries.

Ladies and gentlemen, I was thrilled to receive a subpoena to appear before the Western Australian Royal Commission this week. I had been going out to the mail box every morning for the past six months and returning glum and empty-handed. But now that the bluey has come registered mail from WA I can't wait to get into that room before the big three, climb in the box and spill my guts in a desperate bid to clear my name and that of the Slaven Nelson Group.

I want to take a few moments here today in the Toth to outline my defence. I have nothing to hide. But, my very good friends, I am sick of the snide innuendo whenever I pull up for a tank of unleaded and four litres of oil at the local garage. I am sick of the continual sniggering and racy gags about my fishing trips and collection of antiques and artworks. Make no mistake, ladies and gentlemen. My red-hot testimony will shock a lot of people. I don't shy away from the fact that there are millions missing . . . no, as you were . . . there are *billions* missing from the Slaven Nelson Group and the coffers of the nation.

I don't try and hide the truth about the after-hours parties in the Player's Credit Union headquarters, Lithgow, where the Jatz, the soft cheese, the individually wrapped king prawns airlifted in by the tonne from Thailand, the Brett Whiteley Chardonnay and the Mark Rothko Grange Hermitage never ran out. It's true that the hosties and artists' models were flown in from all over Australia and the South Pacific once the balloon that a do was on went up and cleared the mezzanine level of the atrium of our lavish HQ. The art works were expensive and often we paid a lot more than the going rate. But when you want the best, luxury doesn't have a price—just ask Chris Skase. The music was loud, the jokes were blue but the bottom line always, ladies and gentlemen, was that business was done.

This is true of the so-called fishing trip when myself, my partner Rampaging Roy Slaven, our bagman Mungo 'Chooka' Willessee, Rupert Murdoch, the then PM Bobby Hawke and a couple of friends we met at one of the Credit Union parties set off from Port Kembla for a week's fishing.

You can laugh, if you like, at our lack of success with the rod and reel. To the best of my recollection the PM bagged a couple of leatherjackets which we gutted and threw back hoping to lure a big white to the eighteen-foot runabout. I got amongst a school of mullet and Roy filled the boat with tuna. But we were there in the Tasman Sea to thrash out elements of a media and property package with roots on three continents and to get away from the office hurly-burly for a day or two of gags, of nude swimming in shark-infested waters and of living off the freezer full of grub. I came back absolutely refreshed and went to work with a renewed vigour.

205

Isn't it so easy in these days of fiscal rectitude to point the crooked finger at the creative business practices of yesteryear and call foul and scream excess, as my critics do. However, there are questions that need answers. For instance, the WA Royal Commission would love to know the exact whereabouts of the Slaven Nelson Group's chief accountant during the years 1984 through 1988. But I ask you, as I have asked myself a thousand times, is it likely that a knight of the realm would be on the fiddle trying to get the better of a nation that welcomed him as one of their own, after a run of financial outs in England and Europe?

I also agree that it would be fanastic if Sir Pranger could return from his isolated retreat in a Buddhist monastery in northern Burma to answer delicate cash flow questions. But Snoodie has always been an intensely religious man, and has taken the opportunity of this current downturn in the business scene to become more acquainted with the inner world of spiritual matters where desires and material possessions are simply baggage from an earlier life. He has gone to Burma to become more acquainted with the landscape and light. And the trip seems to be paying dividends. Pranger has already committed himself to knocking out an exhibition of forty-five canvases on his return. From the black and white photostats they look absolute crackers.

I will address other matters before the Commission, like my so-called unwise investment of government funds in the arts. Friends, it is true I invested a fortune in an antique collection of empty wine bottles, quilts and Holden hubcaps. I agree I paid top dollar for what has turned out to be a worthless heap of rubbish. But you have to remember the volatile pre-crash days of mid-'87 when even pre-war railway sleepers were being sold at Sotheby's for 270 times their original price. I made the bottle and hubcap investments hoping to present my collection to the nation at an appropriate date. Is it now my fault that this collection is stored in the Northside tip left out unprotected in all weather? And what of the extensive bills I ran up on the telephone while away on government business trying to establish the rugby league as an export industry across Indonesia, Malaysia and as far north as Macao? I agree $37,500 on phone bills and post-age in three

206

weeks is a substantial wedge out of the government purse and it does, with the certainty of twenty-twenty hindsight, seem a little excessive. But why can't a keen punter keep track of Cup hopes, collect the late mail from the stables and ring around the bookies to get the best odds? After all, I thought that was what free enterprise was all about.

Lastly, what of this major charge against me? I do not shy away from the fact that I received $13.7 million as a fee from the on-selling of a dud, disused Lithgow petrol station site to the Federal Government in late 1986. But when you had the elaborate plans, the breathtaking vision for Australia that was pouring out of Canberra in those days, my end of the deal was dirt cheap. Simply a snack on the side left there for the mice.

I know this may sound strange but I still feel as though I was not adequately compensated for my time that week. When I consider the introductions, the loan of my office for an afternoon, access to a telephone, fax and photocopying facilities, the secretarial assistance for the best part of a morning, local knowledge, a light lunch, the use of the car for the delicate negotiations away from prying ears, and getting the principals together in the first place, that had to be worth something. After all, I would have been an idiot to myself and the business community to give all that away free. Am I now to be pilloried for my part in what one authoritative financial writer at the time declared the deal of the century?

I leave you to be the judge, grateful that I have had this chance to present the facts here in the comfort of the Laszlo Toth Room.

RACING - THE WAY TO GET THEM BACK

And now let's leave the world of business and art far behind and tackle something which everyone is concerned about—the collapse of the racing industry. Let's look forward to a brighter future.

Let's face it, friends and fellow punters, the world has not been kind to racing in 1991. And it's good to see a number of keen punters and club secretaries here in the Toth this morning. Prize money is down. Tracks are closing. The public is staying away. The bookies are on the squeal. The TAB is looking for exotic scams for pinching the public's money. Club secretaries are at the end of their tether setting themselves for the high jump. Sponsors are looking elsewhere. It is a sorry picture. But all need not be doom and gloom and in the few moments left to us I want to make two simple suggestions, absolutely free of charge, to club committees. They are a radical but workable solution to racing's current problems and will take the caper into the twenty-first century in a doddle.

Improvement number one, the

Celebrity Shooter Program. Picture this, you club secretaries in the audience desperate to see more punters banging over the turnstiles at your track. A nude celebrity is engaged to be on hand for each race meeting in the metropolitan area and the closer country meets.

The personality, let's say it's Zsa Zsa Gabor (who I know for a fact loves racing and shooting), passes the afternoon leaning on the club's twelve-gauge double-barrel shotgun camped at the gate of the mounting enclosure. Zsa Zsa passes the day with her adoring public signing autographs, telling gags and dishing out the informed late mail. In race four there is a pile-up and a promising three-year-old breaks down at the point of the turn. The stewards call for the screens after the course vet has made the examination and signalled the very worst.

Ms Gabor swings into action. She shoulders arms and strolls the five hundred metres down the track to the fallen conveyance, waving to the crowd, with the shooting implement at a jaunty rack over her shoulder James Dean-style. Zsa Zsa arrives at the tragic scene, ducks behind the screens and does the business with the fire stick—a big bang

● ● ●

and a cloud of smoke. Cheers go up from the packed stands. Zsa Zsa emerges smiling from ear to ear giving the waiting press and shooting groupies the thumbs up. She proceeds to answer a barrage of questions from the press and TV news crews like, 'What was it like in there, Zsa Zsa?', 'Was it a living hell, Ms Gabor?', 'Will you be back for the Windsor and Newton Cup next year?'

The stewards then draw the screens back so as kiddies can have their photos taken with Ms Gabor and the fallen but still warm conveyance. The course artist whips up a six-by-twelve-inch picture of the scene for the clubhouse. Don't tell me that families, mums and dads and boys and girls would not be queuing at the gate hours before the first race, especially if word was strategically leaked to the press that, say, Johnny Depp, AFL star Tony Lockett, Abigail, Collette, Bernard King or Kylie and Jason were booked to be in action nude trackside at that afternoon's big eight-race card. Talk about giving the public memories that they would pass on to their grandchildren and get the youth of the nation thinking of racing in the nicest and most positive way.

My second suggestion is a series of Nude Race Days. Once again, club secretaries, take a moment and imagine the whole W.S. Cox Plate meeting going off a treat without a stitch of clothing in sight. Punters, as they arrive and tog off in their cars, would be soaking up informed comment from TAB stations around the nation and following the tips of a nude Maxie Presnell, Ron Papps, Brian Martin or Wayne Wilson. As they stroll through the gates in the raw shelling out hard-earned as an admission, they would be assessing the thoughts of Dave Tootell, Jim Cassidy, Damien Oliver or Brian York about the coming day's book of nude rides.

The mounting enclosure would be a riot of human colour and mad action as nude punters would be swapping late mail with nude journos, nude jockeys would be taking their instructions from nude trainers, and nude socialites would be trying to get the leg-up from nude connections. The Fourth Military District Band would be blazing away nude on classics like 'I Touch Myself', 'Like a Virgin' and 'Staying Alive' out front of the Hayden Haitana Stand full of nude families having the time of their life. Out back in the ring, nude bookies would be knocked over in the rush by nude form students, and nude touts would be making desperate bids to get on early at succulent odds. The nude police would have a very quiet day as there would be not a dip or pickpocket in sight because quite simply there would be no pockets on course. Nude club officials would be able to take the afternoon off as no-one would be breaking the dress code by turning up with the wrong length of sock or wearing the wrong coat in the members'. Imagine the sight as the horses swing for home in the feature race, the crowd rising as one, the big punters, nude, seeing a dream come true and unable to hide their emotions, the connections who normally throw their hats in the air having to make do with race books as they get excited and begin hugging one another, getting aroused in the nicest possible way in the members' stand. Think of the photo opportunities as the excitement and champagne flows with everyone buffed up as nude as the day they were born. It would be a day so free of the problems that beset modern racing and so healthy for all concerned. The winning thing about these ideas is that they would cost nothing to organise apart from a couple of phone calls. And who knows, if we really put our minds to it we may be able to effect both between now and Cup Day this year.

Just finally, I see by the program that you're headed down to the NSW Art Gallery later today. Get Fast Eddie to tell you his Kandinski gags. He has a couple of rippers—very blue, very French and very Edmund. And as you leave Eddie on the steps remember to make him an offer for anything apart from the Kandinskis.

• •

Thanks very much for your attention – and happy conferencing.

The *Social Set* -
Tennis Afterhours

It still amazes everyone I meet that our first Pat, Pat Cash, won Wimbledon in 1987. How did he climb that mountain so easily? Since then he has given the world so much more. His tennis racquet guitar is without peer. He retains all of his phenomenal footspeed. And donating his knees and buttocks to science is a gesture that we, as a nation, still don't fully appreciate. I've got my hat and my pants off to the bloke. Australian of the Century? My vote – Cash, P.

Last Sunday night was the big gig for the tennis world when the players, umpires and officials had a chance to lift the toupees and wig out before the hostilities commenced for the 1990 All England crown.

The whole tennis tour packed the London Hard Rock Cafe dressed to score. Everyone was there—Steffi, Martina, Zina, Gabriela, Stefan, Brod, Brad and Fitzy. Steffi's dad Pete was lurking up the back amongst the ferns and the only sadness of the night was the knowledge that Teddy Tingling wouldn't be bobbing in round midnight to wish everyone all the best.

The Cafe had slipped itself out back behind the swinging kitchen doors and threw at us a seafood cocktail, followed up by a choice between mince on toast and chicken Kiev, with a chocolate mousse ● ● ● ●

213

dessert and a whip round the room from the cheese and Jatz platter. All this was chased past the laughing gear by a couple of smoky whites, and a case of Hardy's Old Cave Port before the liqueurs were broken out from the top shelf. It got the evening off to a great start.

Then round 10.30 pm the tables were pushed back and clambering up on the planks at the far end of the Pancho Gonzales Room was the bunch of cool rocking hombres with a just a hint of moustache drooping from the upper lip. This serve and volley gang was headed up by John McEnroe, who had thrown the combo together with Vitas Gerulaitas and Pat Cash on guitars, while bashing away down in the engine room was the Mac himself on bass and Boom Boom Becker on the drums. The Mac really puts out on these occasions, rehearsing for weeks, and it's easy to say now that he has dipped out in round one, that he put a little too much into the night but, hey, that's just the way he is.

John got the gang cooking and Cashy kicked off the night with an Aerosmith medley including a knock-out version of 'Dude (Looks Like a Lady)' which had everyone on their feet doing the twist. Then John stepped up to the mike and thrilled the mod crowd with his forty-five minute reading of the Stones' tennis classic, 'You Can't Always Get What You Want'.

The spotlight swung Boris's way and he grabbed the mike and belted out a fabulous hard-rocking version of 'I Should Be So Lucky'. At half-time the Hoad and Rosewall Show took over and these two old stagers proved once again that you are only as young as you feel when they whipped up a storm with an acoustic bracket of old Australian favourites like JPY's 'Where the Action Is' and the autobiographical 'Yesterday's Hero'.

The surprise of the night was an a cappella version of the AC/DC tune 'It's a Long Way To the Top If You Want To Rock'n'Roll' from Steffi, Monica, Jennifer and Gabriela. This was their encore after singing their way through at least twenty hits requested from the audience.

The only awkward moment of the evening came at the end of the second set when Cashy was strutting his stuff in a frenzy on the fretboard during the solo from the old heavy metal chestnut 'Smoke On the Water'. He was doing his Pete Townshend impersonation, jumping up and down and swinging the arm like a windmill. It's a fabulous routine that had the crowd screaming for more. Pat, with his headband ablaze, took off for his twenty-seventh big jump and crashed back to the planks with the Slazenger Stratocaster six-string jammed between the crutch of his shorts and a large knothole in the floor. He was suspended there, stuck, screaming in agony. Everyone fell about laughing, thinking it was part of the act. It was only quick work from Vitas who belted the guitar away with his own axe that saved Pat from permanent injury. I gave him what assistance I could, applying the sugarbag full of hot sand that I always carry in the back of the ute in case I happen upon an accident scene. I'm sure that the accident aggravated the nagging groin injury that slowed him up in his opening round. Pat was a bit groggy but he saw the set through.

Then it was all back to Newk's place, which is two doors up from the Centre Court, for the annual 'Australians at home in Wimbledon' barbeque. By the time we got there Newk and Fiery Fred Stolle had the coals glowing and a nice forequarter of hogget dripping on the spit, with a couple of hot trays groaning under lamb grillers and the Roy Slaven signature smallgoods specially turned out in the Wimbledon colours.

IT WAS CERTAINLY A NIGHT TO REMEMBER and the perfect way to kick off a fortnight of the greatest tennis comp in the world. The only face from the seeds that was missing was Ivan Lendl's. The big man wasn't there. In a desperate bid to bag the All England on grass, Ivan has created a routine and atmosphere just like home. He has built a mock-up of his house in a suburb of London which re-creates in every detail the patch where he hangs out Stateside. Everything is there – the shops, the used car lots, the bread he likes. The papers are delivered exactly as they are at home, and even the postie who brings the letters has been flown in for the fortnight. With all this on his mind it's no wonder he can't forget the game for a night and relax.

What Was I Doing When Gatum Gatum Won the Cup?

I am often asked by business boards I sit on to cough up a cv which can be used to persuade gun-shy investors that I am the man for the job and more than a useful replacement for the well-credentialled knight who just couldn't make the meetings because of terminal gout. This cv got me work on the boards of Westpac and General Electric, onto the selection committee at the Carlton Football Club, it secured a spot as chairman of the Crown Casino Entertainment appointments committee and into the UN head office in New York as Unicef's bigwig. Feel free to copy it and call it your own. ● ● ● ● ● ●

receding falcon

FAVOURITE MATTRESS: the King Tide Sleepmaker.

'You get the sleep of the dead on a mattress full of flathead.'

FAVOURITE MAGAZINE: Trot Guide.

If the Trots are giving you the trots, don't be snide, read Trot Guide.

FAVOURITE ABATTOIR: the Lithgow Abattoir.

Lithgow, where they're doing things with meat butchers have only dreamed of.

FAVOURITE BANK: the Lithgow Bank.

The only bank in the history of money to combine nudity and football.

FAVOURITE TOILET: the Julian McMahon Toilet.

On the Julian there is so much more room for the hips.

FAVOURITE BOOK: The Killer in Jodhpurs by Lady Colin Campbell.

The unauthorised biography of Prince Philip.

FAVOURITE HOLIDAY SPOT: Nude Island.

Where you have never felt so free.

FAVOURITE MEAL:

ENTRÉE—cream nuts drizzled in a fist-blown flute and mango sauce;
MAIN—breadcrumbed marinated tuft with seasonal vegetables;
DESSERT—sticky date pudding.

FAVOURITE TINNED FRUIT: the SPC Two Fruits in Lite Syrup.

FAVOURITE CAR: the 1989 Zil first; daylight second; the Nissan Cedric a fast-finishing third.